POLICY STUDIES IN EMPLOYMENT AND WELFARE NUMBER 25

General Editor: Sar A. Levitan

Auto Work and Its Discontents

Edited by B. J. Widick

Foreword by Eli Ginzberg

The Johns Hopkins University Press, Baltimore and London

Manufactured in the United States of America

The Johns Hopkins University Press, Baltimore, Maryland 21218
The Johns Hopkins Press Ltd., London

Library of Congress Catalog Card Number 76—16095
ISBN 0—8018—1856—7 (cloth)
ISBN 0—8018—1857—5 (paper)

Library of Congress Cataloging in Publication data will be found on the last printed page of this book.

Contents

Foreword   Eli Ginzberg   vii

Introduction   B. J. Widick   1

1. Work in Auto Plants: Then and Now   B. J. Widick   6

2. A Feminist Union Perspective   Patricia Cayo Sexton   18

3. The Skilled Trades: Reflections   Bill Goode   34

4. Alienation and Dehumanization?   Robert Reiff   45

5. Black Workers: Double Discontents   B. J. Widick   52

6. Job Satisfaction: A Critique   Al Nash   61

7. Summary and Conclusions   B. J. Widick   89

Epilogue: Working Conditions and Managements' Interests   Ivar Berg   96

Biographical Notes   108

Bibliography   Al Nash   109

Tables

1. Occupational Distribution in Michigan's Transportation Equipment Industry   24

2. Thirteen Major Studies or Articles About Assembly-Line Auto Workers   64

Foreword

The last years, that is, before the worldwide recession of 1974 shifted the focus back to job security, witnessed a burgeoning interest in a subject that has come to be known as the quality of working life. Scholars, employers, labor leaders, journalists, and politicians rediscovered the theme of work satisfaction or, better, work dissatisfaction, the causes and the cures. The principal actor in this revival was Lordstown, Ohio, the newly constructed, highly automated GM plant that was programmed to produce Vegas at the rate of over one hundred per hour. A long and bitter strike was interpreted by the media as the revolt of young workers against the intolerable conditions of their work exemplified by the speed of the line, the repetitive nature of their tasks, the tight discipline, and the difficulties of their progressing into less-pressured jobs—an updated version of Charles Chaplin's *Modern Times*.

Once the strike was settled, little more was heard of Lordstown, at least in the media. But concern with the quality of working life was not dissipated. Senator Edward Kennedy held hearings; Professors Louis Davis and Albert Cherns sponsored an international conference at Arden House, the results of which have just been published in two volumes, *The Quality of Working Life;* selective interest in management and trade-union circles continued to be manifest; and still other groups poked at the subject in an effort to discern whether one or another form of intervention could lead to increased worker satisfaction, higher productivity, and an improvement in the industrial environment.

My colleague, B. J. Widick, discussed with me the proposal out of which the present monograph stems and sought my assistance in having it funded by the Ford Foundation that earlier had provided support for several explorations of the subject. He had the ingenious idea of eliciting the cooperation of a group of scholars, each one of whom had earlier had a minimum of three years' experience in an auto plant; had served as a union plant bargaining agent; and had retained an interest in the industry, the union, and the workers.

Widick believed that if he could persuade his colleagues to engage in a collaborative "remembrance of things past" from their present vantage and with the deepening insights produced by their several scholarly disciplines, the subject would be illuminated far beyond the treatment afforded it by management consultants looking for a fee or journalists looking for a lead story.

Unlike many good ideas that remain stillborn, Widick was able to carry this one through to completion, as a result of which the public, lay and professional, has in my view the first balanced treatment of a subject that is as important as it is illusive, a subject that has been victimized by having been studied by investigators whose ideological commitments misdirected their attention and confounded their treatment of the evidence.

This small book has many virtues. It is written by people who know, firsthand, what they are writing about. The authors are sensitive to the economic and technological commitments under which automobiles are produced without falling into the trap of utopians or apologists who see no prospect for improvement. They deal with workers as real people, not symbols in a class struggle. They do not hide the fact that workers, like other people, include racists, drug addicts, alcoholics. Morever, the authors see the workers whole—what transpires in the plant is not unrelated to the problems that workers leave behind in the morning and return to in the evening.

While this book is not a mystery, I think it best that the reader discover for himself where the authors came out after their successful effort at group recollection and reassessment. I will encourage him to find out by noting that the tale is well told and that the ending, in my view, comes closer to the truth than any other treatment of a theme that has confused social scientists since the days of Karl Marx.

October 1975   Eli Ginzberg
                                          Columbia University

Introduction

The idea for this book arose from a sense of frustration over the debate and literature about blue-collar work and its discontents, in particular in the automobile industry. It developed into a project when I contacted friends in academia who had a background of years in auto plants and union bargaining experience, and had maintained a keen interest and concern about their shopmates and the organization that represented them in collective bargaining—the United Auto Workers union (UAW).

Under the aegis of the Ford Foundation, and with the encouragement of Eli Ginzberg, I was able to form a team of five individuals whose unique experiences provided the possibility of a fresh look and judgment on the subject of auto work and its discontents. Through close association I knew that Al Nash for the past two years was an active contributor to that major project of *Work, Productivity and Job Satisfaction* by Raymond A. Katzell, Daniel Yankelovich, et al., supported by the National Science Foundation. We had served as chief stewards together in an auto plant. Nash represented the motor line, and I functioned in the trim assembly shop. We had discussed the nature of grievances, speedup, and job problems ad infinitum. Nash agreed to review the major research and findings on these subjects. His shortened work paper and his ten years of plant experience were an invaluable contribution to our project. Then we enlisted Patricia Cayo Sexton, the sociologist, whose four books on blue-collar workers and minorities are recognized as first-rate. Pat Sexton was a pioneer in union, civil, and women's rights struggles—long before it was chic. She worked on an assembly line for two years and was an elected chief steward at the Dodge Main Plant—not an easy position in what was known as "The Polish Local" in 1946. Her working paper provides experiences, views, and insights difficult to find in any of the usual studies about women and work. Robert Reiff was once a welder in a metal shop at Chrysler, then a chief steward, and finally a professional psychologist (Ph.D.), specializing for many years in the field of mental health problems of blue-collar workers. For a time he was a consultant to the UAW. His critical comments about theories and his personal experiences, as reflected upon, gave another invaluable input into our project. A major area usually neglected in most literature is the skilled trades, and the UAW has over one hundred fifty thousand skilled workers. For our project we obtained Bill Goode, associate dean of the Empire State Labor College, to look into their problems and discuss his own experiences. Goode spent ten years as a pipefitter and committeeman at Ford Highland Park. Later he was a labor educator and eventually directed labor education at Wayne State University before coming to New York. His working paper expands the perspective of our work.

Fifteen years of my life were spent in the Chrysler-Jefferson-Kercheval plant—lately in the national news media as a symbol of the auto industry's distress with the threat of its permanent closing down. My writings (three books and innumerable articles in magazines as diverse as *Dissent,* the *Nation,* the *New Republic,* and the *Columbia Journal of World Business*) reflect this indelible experience—something my colleagues in this project also felt. I have kept in touch with my friends in the plant ever since. I toured other plants here and abroad to keep my knowledge of plant conditions up-to-date. This is summarized in my working paper.

Finally, there was a need to emphasize a largely overlooked factor of discontent—usually written about only in the radical

2

press with its predetermined biases. That is the question of the status of the blacks, then and now—seldom included in the studies about job satisfaction. Way back in 1955, Walter Reuther hired me to do a study of the problems of blacks in the auto industry and their relations to the union. I interviewed fifteen outstanding black leaders (both pro- and anti-Reuther) in depth. The results were never published, but I used the notes for background. As an active participant in the campaign organized by Horace Sheffield, Robert Battles III, and the late Willoughby Abner to break the barrier against blacks in the top leadership of the UAW, I spent much time writing, working, and defending myself in this struggle which predated the civil rights movement and was not always a pleasant experience. The working paper speaks for itself on this issue.

After exchanging working papers and critical comments, our team held a weekend seminar in May 1975 at Columbia University's Arden House. It featured an intense and lively exchange of views, not even interrupted by meals in the dining room. Theories and viewpoints were argued not in the polite language of a cloistered ivory-tower gathering but in the vigorous style of UAW debate—quite uninhibited. It was intellectually stimulating and personally exciting. Out of it came a meeting of the minds that would need more reflection for certainty of views and judgments. Again we exchanged views and draft proposals for a summary by each participant. Out of this emerged a common document of summary conclusions.

This report is bound to raise more issues and controversy—so the authors intend. Neither the protagonists of job satisfaction nor of alienation theories are likely to accept the challenge to their basic assumptions contained in our conclusions:

> In reflecting on the realities of workers' attitudes and social relations in the auto factory, and in reviewing the variety and complexity of problems and sources of friction and anxieties which exist there, the participants concluded that neither a hypothesis based on the concepts of "job satisfaction" nor "alienation" alone offered a satisfactory basis for analysis and judgment. Neither approaches factors in the totality of and the wide differences in the causes of job discontents, nor the many variables which affect workers in the auto

3

industry. The feelings of most workers about their jobs tend to form a continuum between job satisfaction and alienation rather than polarization around either concept.

The concepts of "job satisfaction" or of "alienation" do not offer a satisfactory explanation for the degree of conflict, change, or challenge found in the workplace environment. Studies based on those concepts do not explain the existence of the auto union and its impact and its struggles, or the problems growing out of the heterogeneous and changing composition of the work force, or the effect of social, economic, and political events on the work force.

Nor is our conclusion about viewpoints toward auto workers likely to please some critics or academics.

The participants state candidly:

Finally, it must be added that in our experience and study we found no evidence that the auto workers are either robots or dehumanized, nor are they a combination of satisfied robots and ignorant Archie Bunkers. Their prejudices and outlook generally reflect those of other segments of American society.

And they do have a grievance against society, with its middle class values, and that is the general contempt in which factory workers, in particular assembly line workers, are held, making it doubly difficult for blue collar workers to maintain a sense of personal pride and dignity. Even among skilled workers in auto plants, there is often a feeling of superiority over the assembly line or unskilled worker. And those who see workers as robots or Archie Bunkers, also contribute to the antagonisms, irritations and frustrations of the people who work for a living in the auto factories.

The main thrust of our views is concentrated in the summary conclusions, for which a reading of the working papers provides the appropriate background.

Two final points:

Our friendly but critical view of the limitations of unionism as a problem-solving institution may displease some of our former colleagues in the United Auto Workers union, but no more than our judgment on management's role may raise temperatures in auto circles.

If, as the participants expect, these are the indicated reactions to our views, the work of this team of research-scholars was worth the time and effort; especially if scholars, managers, and labor leaders who profess a similar concern for the blue-collar workers now address the many unresolved challenges and problems summarized in this report.

B. J. Widick
Editor and Project Director

1

Work in Auto Plants: Then and Now

B. J. Widick

In our book, *The UAW and Walter Reuther,* Irving Howe and I wrote a section called "Fighting the Line," which is a standard intellectual approach to what was wrong with assembly-line work based on my personal experiences at the Chrysler Jefferson-Kercheval Plant. We argued that assembly-line work was deadly boring and created a psychology which we called "fighting the line."

To explain, we wrote:

> The whole point of assembly-line production can be summarized in one word: rationalization. If, for example, there are 100 operations to be performed, ten men trained to perform ten operations each can do the job in, say, x units of time. But if 100 men are available they can each be trained to do one simplified operation, with the result that their speed is increased and the total unit of time for doing the job may be cut to three-fourths, say, of the time it took before. Though simplified, this example does illustrate the way rationalization of production and the division of labor works out. In terms of production: efficiency; in terms of the human being: depersonalization, robotization, and a sense of alienation from the total productive process.

Furthermore,

> The inexorable flow of the bodies or motors along the assembly lines gives the workers a sense of constant pre-occupation which makes relaxation almost impossible. One feels oneself becoming a function of an impersonal apparatus—and do not think that simply because most workers are unable to articulate this feeling that they do not have it! They may just say "it's driving me nuts," but in those four simple words is a profound psychological problem reaching the very heart of industrial civilization.
>
> Sometimes the men on the line try to get time for "a break" by moving "up the line." This means that they work very quickly so as to move ahead to future units of work before the momentum of the assembly line would require them to. In this way they may gain five or ten minutes for a smoke. But soon enough the line catches up with you (it never seems to get tired) and you have to fulfill its demands. Sometimes you may fall behind and bang a hammer on a piece of steel or shout for the "utility man" in order to get some help. But move "up the line" or fall behind it, the assembly line worker is deprived of one precious privilege that the skilled worker still enjoys: that of setting, within any small unit of time, his own pace of work even though he may consequently have to work harder later on.
>
> Soon the auto worker gets the feeling the men in the plants sometimes call "fighting the line," which might best be described as a mixture of punch-drunk and city-tense. Implicitly rejecting the idea that he is merely a function of a mechanical process, the worker tries to rebel against it; but not only doesn't the assembly line recognize his rebellion, it even refuses to recognize his separate identity. The psychological result is that the worker's aggression against the line can be released only against himself or other workers.[1]

Frankly, I was influenced greatly by Charles Chaplin's movie *Modern Times*, which depicted an assembly-line worker becoming a robot in his automatic reflexes as he worked on the line. Of course, then and even now, most writers dealing with the auto industry fail to recognize that less than 20 percent of the auto workers do work on assembly lines. General Motors, for example, has 110 plants, of which only 24 are passenger car and truck assembly plants, and its total employment is over 550,000 people. Ford Motor Company has 17 assembly plants as compared to 44 manufacturing plants and 32 parts distribution centers. Ford employs over 200,000. Chrysler has 59 plants, of which only 8 are assembly type. It employs about 140,000 people. [2]

For an overview of the auto industry work content, General Motors' 1974 figures provide some valuable insights. Its total average employment in the United States was 555,578. In terms of job categories (as defined by the Bureau of Labor Statistics) GM had a total of 140,130 white-collar employees—49,800 of them were officials and managers; 31,848 were professionals; 12,516 were technicians; 4,777 were sales workers; and 41,189 were office and clerical workers.

In the so-called blue-collar category, 89,091 were skilled craftsmen; 294,402 were operatives (semiskilled); 16,452 were laborers (unskilled); and 15,503 were service workers. Out of the total blue-collar work force, not more than 25 percent could be classified as assembly-line workers, according to both union and industry estimates. [3]

As a matter of fact, it was not until my third year in an auto assembly plant, when I was elected chief steward and got off the line, that I realized that in an assembly plant a maximum of 75 percent of the workers worked on the lines. The over 25 percent who did not included the skilled trades and maintenance men and a large number of material handlers, inspectors, repairmen, sewing machine operators (all women), and persons handling feeder operations from minor assembly.

The point is that most auto workers do not work on assembly lines, and the image of assembly-line work as symbolic of the total character of auto industry factory life is misleading, and, more important, inadequate as a focus for studying the quality of workplace problems.

Ignored, for example, was this issue. Early in 1975, the governor of Michigan and the Occupational Safety Standards Commission suspended safety regulations. The Michigan Manufacturers Association commented: "Literally hundreds of our members could not comply with such a standard and remain competitive with other states." The regulations would have required factories to install new presses or to attach automatic feeders on old presses that would keep workers' hands out of the impact area where dies often strike down with tons of force. The UAW reported that four Michigan workers were killed and 621 were severely injured by power press accidents in 1973, the last year for which data was available. Of these 307 were amputations. [4]

In the steel press plants where the hoods and fenders and other parts are stamped out, safety, health, and noise problems have always constituted at least half of the major grievances and causes of walkouts, as a study over a three-year period revealed. (It was made for me by an assistant personnel director of a steel plant as part of his graduate work.) Heat in foundry plants and fumes in paint shop or paint assembly lines have always been a major source of dispute and cause of wildcat strikes as well as grievances.

Until the issue of plant safety and work environments became part of the national debate on environmental questions in the 1970's, the whole area of auto and other industrial problems was largely ignored in the surveys and books about the overall quality of work in this industry. (See Al Nash's critical survey of the literature on the quality of work in the auto industry.)

Largely overlooked in most studies, for example, is any evaluation of an important index of sources of discontent, the number and kind of local demands and plant bargaining involved as part of national contract negotiations. According to figures released by General Motors in their 1973 Bargaining Fact Sheet, the local bargaining at the plant level has become increasingly difficult in recent years. Here are the GM figures on local demands.:

Year	Local demands
1958	11,600
1961	19,000
1964	24,000
1967	31,000
1970	39,000

These local demands cover working conditions, cafeterias, parking lots, locker rooms, local seniority, wage and shift preference agreements, and a variety of other local issues.

These issues must be resolved with 146 local union shop committees. The seriousness of this problem is evidenced by the fact that since 1958 more than one hundred million man-hours have been lost due to strikes over local demands.[5]

Official and unofficial figures indicate that the number of grievances annually processed in General Motors plants is about two hundred fifty thousand, with the majority involving discipline cases.[6] In 1974, according to UAW sources, safety grievances were becoming the majority, with good results for the union. The recent joint union-management safety committees have had a hopeful early response.

The vast increase in local demands and the number of grievances processed annually is attributable, in my view, to the difference in the character of the auto industry work force, compared to the depression-grown older generation of workers. As Malcolm Denise, Ford vice president and industrial relations director, told a nationwide gathering of plant managers in December 1969,

Nowadays employees are (1) less concerned about losing a job or staying with an employer; (2) less willing to put up with dirty and uncomfortable working conditions; (3) less likely to accept the unvarying pace and functions on moving assembly lines; and (4) less willing to conform to rules or be amenable to higher authority.

Furthermore, the traditional U.S. work ethic—the concept that hard work is a virtue and duty—has undergone considerable erosion.

There are two basic causes of the new situation in manufacturing plants which apply to the entire industrial complex:

On the other hand, we have on the hourly employment rolls more of the kind of persons that carry the label "problem employees." These are the people who almost habitually violate our plant rules. Although some of them do so with an open attitude of rebellion and defiance, in a great many other cases it is just a matter of the problem employee bringing with him into the plant the mores of his own background. He continues to follow his own way of life—to live by the loose code he grew up with—and he is generally indifferent to the standards of someone else's society.

While some of the problem employees have come to us through our efforts to hire the so-called "hardcore unemployables," most of them are simply a reflection of the labor market we've been drawing from for our normal hiring during recent years.

The other root cause of our present difficulties with the work force might be termed a general lowering of employees' frustration tolerance. Many employees, particularly the younger ones, are increasingly reluctant to put up with factory conditions, despite the significant improvements we've made in the physical environment of our plants. Because they are unfamiliar with the harsh economic facts of earlier years, they have little regard for the consequences if they take a day or two off.

For many, the traditional motivations of job security, money rewards, and opportunity for personal advancement are proving insufficient. Large numbers of those we hire find factory life so distasteful they quit after only brief exposure to it. The general increase in real wage levels in our economy has afforded more alternatives for satisfying economic needs.

There is also, again especially among the younger employees, a growing reluctance to accept shop discipline. This is not just a shop phenomenon; rather, it is a manifestation in our shops of a trend we see all about us among today's youth. [7]

The life of local union officials, chief stewards, and committeemen has been made much more difficult by this younger generation, and the day-to-day bargaining more intense, but this is hardly the stuff of which headlines are made, except when reflected in a dramatic strike such as Lordstown in 1972. A critical point of contention is, of course, the pace of work, usually resulting in a charge of speedup by the workers, if management attempts to increase the individual workload for whatever the reason.

Work standards departments make a theoretical estimate of the amount of work a man can do in a given period of time and expect men on the assembly line to perform to that standard. At the beginning of each model, manpower is allocated according to the theoretical framework but, of course, the standard is not achieved immediately because of production difficulties. The assembly lines gradually increase their speed as the production difficulties are overcome, until a maximum of projected cars an hour roll off the end of the final OK line. If each man or woman on the various assembly lines sees his workload increasing, the natural tendency is to complain about speedup. In the 1950's, in my plant and in many auto plants and at union gatherings and conventions, the questions of speedup had top priority. As late as 1964, Walter Reuther described auto plants as "gold plated sweat shops."

The pace of work, that is, the amount of actual physical effort a man or woman had to put into performing an operation, was in 1949, and remains today, a source of constant dispute. The most dramatic, recent example is the Lordstown strike in 1972, which I described in the *Nation* on March 27, 1972:

> The site of the dipute is Lordstown, Ohio, part of the Cleveland-Warren industrial complex. The plant is GM's new, highly automated Vega assembly operation. This plant and the Vega were to be GM's answers to small imports. The factory has been designed to turn out 100 vehicles an hour. The Vega is put together from 578 different body parts; the average car, by contrast, has 996. This reduction, plus the latest automated equipment, seemed to make the compact a sure manufacturing success.

> As further assurance, GM carefully screened its work applicants (to avoid problem employees—BJW), seeking and obtaining mainly young (average age less than 25), white workers with a better than average education (more years of high school). Less than 500 of the plant employees are women and only 100 are black. The pay scale is about $36 a day, not counting fringe benefits. Relief time is about twenty-three minutes twice a day. Only a year ago, GM wrote its Vega employees a letter thanking them for a job well done.

> What factors changed this relationship? The passage of time alone turned the excitement of new jobs into the humdrum of assembly line drudgery. Furthermore, GM never achieved its goal of 100 cars per hour off the assembly line, which meant that the work pace never met the arbitrary standards set by GM's time-study engineers. Last October, therefore, GM placed the Vega plant under the control of its General Motors Assembly Division (GMAD), which soon began eliminating or changing jobs and increasing workloads.

> Leonard Woodcock, president of the UAW, remarked recently that GMAD is "probably the roughest, toughest division in GM. They admit they jerked 300 workers out of the system; our people say 700. The men are fighting back. That's all." For management, the issue soon became one of prestige as well as work output. GMAD's

reputation was at stake, and that is one factor in the inability of the two parties to negotiate the grievances peacefully and satisfactorily. Before GMAD took over, there had been 300 grievances; under the new management there were more than 5,000 with hundreds of discipline cases to boot.

GMAD's operational techniques are standard in the auto industry. Works standards engineers determine the number of seconds required for an operation and foremen are given the manpower to perform at that rate. Failure to meet the standard results in disciplinary action against the employee; being sent home, given days off, ultimately discharge. As men resist in one form or another, usually not meeting the workload, the cars go down the line incomplete. When repairs have piled up to a predetermined point, management sends the entire work force home. The key to understanding this performance conflict is that the assembly line determines the pace of the men, not the other way around. Hence workers feel manacled to the line.

In management theory, when "send homes" have occurred a number of times, the men not working directly on the line and thus unaffected by the works standards dispute will begin to put pressure on the assembly workers. "We need the pay; write a grievance. Let's not lose all our power in small fights." This attitude, plus disciplinary measures, is expected to break the resistance to the new works standards, which have been "scientifically" calculated and must therefore be "right." Frequently this process fails, and management faces and accepts a strike, which usually ends in compromise. Then management begins the whole process over again. (That is a thumbnail history of all auto assembly plants.) 8

This constant dispute over work standards (speedup in the eyes of the workers) explains both historically and currently the creation and function of the union as an organization needed to challenge management's attempts to gain extra labor from its work force. (In theory, the annual improvement productivity factor in auto contracts gives union workers annual wage increases based on higher productivity without extra human effort—and this is what most workers challenge. They argue that most work standards programs seek to get the extra effort.) That is still an unresolved question and is reflected in the many authorized and unauthorized strikes that occur over this issue.

While Lordstown was getting the headlines, the Norwood plant was engaged in a 180-day strike with work standards as a central issue.

In many cases during my days in the plant, and as acknowledged by some Lordstown strikers, workers both in the assembly line and in most manufacturing plants, try to beat the system by devising ways to perform their assigned workload and yet find free time. As higher-echelon management and work standards department personnel find these "soft spots" they attempt to increase the workload, on the theory that a man should be working at all times except during his stated relief period. This is another source of friction.

During the 1946-60 period in which I worked in the Chrysler Jefferson-Kercheval plant, the nightmare of job loss through the increase in automation was introduced into the lives of auto workers and increased their anxieties and tensions. This was an added dimension to the constant layoffs and callbacks either because of production changes or the heavier blows of the various recession setbacks. Machine shops, motor lines, press plants, and other manufacturing facilities were more sharply hit by the advent of automation than were assembly plants.

In the 1970's during my frequent visits and interviews in Detroit with union officials, plant bargainers, and rank-and-file members of my old local union, I discovered another source of in-plant discontent, which I had assumed until then was a college campus problem. It was the disturbing drug scene in the auto plants. As Sam Bellomo, vice president of Local 7 and an in-plant bargainer with thirty years' experience stated it: "The boredom on the job? The speed-up? That's routine. What the workers fear most is the drug addict in the plant, both in terms of safety of operations and in the dread of knowing that pushers operate in the plants, and their victims work there. It's not confined to any one group of people. It's the young mainly, both black and white. They don't give a damn about anything." [9]

In retouring the plant, I checked his views with old-timers, foremen, and a former personnel staff man, all of whom confirmed Bellomo's judgment. Drug addicts and drug pushers were a major menace. Fear of them and fear of accidents from hopped-up workers were prevalent. Union staff people agreed privately with my findings. I must add I was also surprised to see how many union officials in the plant and local carried guns for self-protection. Similar findings were disclosed in a *New York Times* survey of the drug problem in the auto industry.[10] As late as April 1975, I was again told by knowledgeable plant people that this terrible situation still existed, affecting plants of all the Big Three, even though both top UAW officials and company men discounted it. Alcoholism, a traditional problem, was higher on their list of priorities for remedial action.

No one seemed disposed to argue against another conclusion I drew in the book *Detroit: City of Race and Class Violence* that the out-plant tensions over race issues in urban areas like Detroit had intensified racial friction within plants and was another painful and negative dimension affecting the quality of work life in the auto industry—the intensity of frictions depending on the ratio of white to black workers in individual plants. Any time either group is a minority, the smaller group resents the majority and its power to determine leadership and representation.[11]

In reflecting on the realities at the workplaces in the auto industry, and reviewing the complexity and variety of the old and new problems, frictions, and fears in factory life, one conclusion seems inescapable: neither a hypothesis of job satisfaction or of alienation offers a sound focal point for analysis and judgment. Both concepts are difficult to define and are too narrow to encompass the totality of variables affecting a worker in an auto plant.

Neither offers satisfactory explanations or a guide for solutions to the conflicts, the incessant changes, and the challenges in the workplace environment. Neither sufficiently takes into account the real or the potential role of the union as a countervailing force to management hierarchy or absolute authority. Nor do these concepts allow for the impact of the changing composition of the work force or the effect of factors outside the workplace on attitudes in the workplace—the social, political, and economic events that impinge on the daily lives of the auto workers. As an example, when Reverend Martin

Luther King was murdered, there were wildcat strikes by blacks in protest and counterwildcat strikes by whites in protest of the American flag flying at half-mast honoring King.

Unquestionably, as Henry Ford II remarked in 1972, "Much of auto industry work is boring but that is also true of factory jobs in many industries." Recently a Lordstown striker returned to the coal mines after his layoff, but declared he was anxiously awaiting a call back to General Motors, a reminder that compared to coal mining, life in an auto plant is preferable. [12] Each issue becomes a matter of comparison.

There have been significant improvements in the physical work environment. Most auto plants are cleaner, neater, with better rest places than twenty-five years ago. Relief time on jobs has reached proportions we once thought were unattainable, given the cost factor involved. The despotism and favoritism of foremen have been muted by the function of the plant bargainers. The system of arbitration has introduced the concept of "just cause" for curbing management behavior—not equal justice to be sure, but a severe modification of total authority and arbitrary action. There is no visible evidence that auto workers are "dehumanized" or mere robots. Any gathering among the hundred fifty thousand UAW retirees testifies to this observation. In all these areas, the union has performed its primary function and has introduced a larger degree of human dignity to auto workers than prevailed in the preunion days. Nevertheless, a vast number of unresolved issues and problems remain.

The many unreported but continuous experiments at the workplace by General Motors to alleviate if not solve the problems reflect the fact that GM management is aware of the challenges confronting it. The UAW raises many work issues constantly, without, of course, having any final answers at its fingertips. Its role is vital, if limited, compared to the power and control of the industry by the industry.

In one area, society itself, with its middle-class value system, is a source of discontent for auto workers, and that is the general contempt with which factory workers, and notably assembly-line workers are viewed, making it doubly difficult to attain a sense

VS.
col
mvng

pride and dignity. Even skilled workers in auto
show a marked disdain for the assembly-line
er unskilled laborer. As for much of the academic
quently expressed view of a blue-collar worker as
of satisfied robot or backward Archie Bunker—
laughs or for someone to feel superior to—adds to
the antagonism, irritation, and frustrations of the people in the
factories.

Notes

1. Irving Howe and B. J. Widick, *The UAW and Walter Reuther* (New York: Random House, 1949), pp. 20–21.
2. Report of the Research Division, Office of Economic Expansion, Michigan Department of Commerce, Lansing, Michigan, "Assembly and Manufacturing Plants of the Motor Vehicle Industry in the United States," June 1972.
3. 1974 General Motors Report on Programs of Public Interest (Detroit: April 1975), table 1, General Motors U.S. Employment at December 31.
4. *Detroit Free Press,* April 15, 1975.
5. General Motors Corporation 1973 Bargaining Fact Sheet, p. 5.
6. Interviews with General Motors and UAW officials, May 1975.
7. Remarks by Malcolm L. Denise, Vice President, Labor Relations, Ford Motor Company at Ford Management Conference, The Greenbrier, White Sulphur Springs, West Virginia, November 10, 1969, pp. 5–6.
8. B. J. Widick, "The Men Won't Toe the Vega Line," *Nation,* 214 (March 27, 1972), 403–74.
9. Personal interviews, June 15, 1971 and January 5, 1975.
10. *New York Times,* June 21, 1971.
11. B. J. Widick, *Detroit: City of Race and Class Violence* (Chicago: Quadrangle Books, 1972), pp. 221–22.
12. *New York Times,* May 4, 1975.

2

A Feminist Union Perspective

Patricia Cayo Sexton

The time was 1946, a long time ago. The place, Dodge Main Plant in Polish Hamtramck, Michigan (now a black ghetto), a big plant of fifteen thousand employees—and me. I applied for a job at Dodge Main and was put without delay on the trim assembly line in an almost all-male department. Why an all-male line, why me? I shall never know. It was then, and still is, a management prerogative to assign new "hires" to any job it pleased. We accepted the assignments without question. Once on the job, we developed a proprietary stake in it. Our interest was in keeping the job we had, not getting a better one. For my part, I was grateful for the assignment. I had lucked out, the job was a good one.

Looking back, it seems likely that they began putting women on the line because they ran out of white men and preferred women to black males. The racial segregation of jobs was not yet an issue. Nor was the sex segregation of jobs. We simply did not question hire-in assignments much. At that time integrating the "greasy spoons" near the shop so that blacks could go out to lunch was as far as we got—a big breakthrough as we saw it. Blacks worked in such nice places as heat treat and foundry, but none had moved into trim. When the movement came, the racial balance tipped quickly. Women never moved in.

During my three years in the shop, I never wore blue collars. Many men wore them, but no women. Like jeans, the blue work shirt was a standard uniform of male factory workers, at least until other options (as T shirts and sport shirts) took over. "Blue collar" is as much a sex stereotype as is "white collar," which is, or was, an office uniform of males but not females. Indeed, so sex-stereotyped has factory work been that even the names of jobs—craftsman, machine repairman, foreman—are masculine. Fortunately, women's liberation and the *Dictionary of Occupational Titles* may change this masculine nomenclature.

In those days, women factory workers had a distinctive dress style, but it was not blue collar. It was pants. Wearing them in public was the equivalent of carrying a black lunch bucket. When you saw a woman on the street in slacks, you knew she worked in a factory and was on her way to or from the job. Nice ladies did not appear in public in slacks, nor did girls dare to wear them to school.

As we know, the postwar generations of middle-class youth, and now even secretaries and Upper East Siders, have gobbled up these high fashions. Females in affluent suburbia put on the workers' slacks and jeans and, in a sense, never took them off.

I like to remember this when I think about the many unrecognized contributions of working-class people to our society. In this case, the contribution was more powerful and lasting than that of *Vogue, Mademoiselle,* and the ten best-dressed women combined. Some day, in this connection, I would like to examine a hypothesis of mine, that almost all unique and positive aspects of our culture (and perhaps other cultures too) originated with these "common" people.

In a department of some five hundred people, only three women worked on the main assembly line. For unexplored reasons, the moving line traditionally has been regarded as a male zone. Women are assigned to desk assembly and small moving lines—which require very little physical movement— but seldom to major assembly. Why this is so is as unclear as the explanations for most sex-linked job categories. In my experience, the moving line—unless it moves too fast—is less demanding than most of the jobs women do. Some tasks on the line are heavy, but most are light and easily mastered by the average woman. Certainly it is more interesting to move around on a line than to stand, or even sit, at a station the whole day, as women often do. Some women don't like it, just as some men don't. But there is nothing intrinsic in most assembly jobs to justify the "for men only" label.

My experience was on the trim line. We did not have to move steel bodies around, and we weren't working with heavy parts or machines. Production standards were relatively humane. That made all the difference. Any job, especially on a moving line, quickly becomes intolerable when production standards are too high. On my job, there was no pressure, little fatigue, and enough time for relaxed kibitzing.

I got one bad taste of high production standards when I was assigned during a layoff to a "woman's job" on a small assembly operation off the main line and physically quite separate from it. It was Chaplinesque and agonizing. I simply could not keep up, or come close to it, even after several weeks. Still, women were doing the job, keeping up, and not complaining. They couldn't understand what was wrong with me, why I couldn't do it. Some even tried to help me pick up my jobs. They didn't know anything better, and most were grateful to have a job at all.

Separate seniority lists were kept for these sex-segregated jobs, so these women could not bump onto the main line during layoffs (and there learn about good production standards), and men from the line could not bump *them* (and perhaps begin to humanize standards on these jobs). During my tenure as chief steward in the department, we tried to combine the seniority lists, but both the men and women resisted. The old story: cling to what you have. A bird in the hand is worth dozens in the bush. Now the lists are merged, I am told.

Production has also been sped up, I learn, to a point just this side of endurance. In my time, we were lucky to have inherited standards set by the reputedly most militant workers in the plant, the "trimmers," the tack-spitters, the men (no women) who tacked up the upholstery trim inside the car.

These experienced men, white and predominantly Polish, were always ready to walk off the job when standards were threatened. Like other skilled workers, they could afford to be tougher than the typical assembler. They had a skill, and they could not be replaced easily. Moreover, because they were skilled, they were more a group than the rest of us—almost a cadre—held together by a common task, identity, interaction— more highly paid, closely knit, better unionized—and more able to act together than unskilled workers.

These trimmers pretty much set, and held, the standards for the rest of us. In the rest of the plant, we in trim were regarded as prima donnas and hotheads. In fact, other parts of the plant got quite tired and angry about being dragged off their jobs so often by trim wildcat strikes. Our response was always: "Do the same for yourselves!" Production standards are hard to deal with job by job or department by department. The strategy divides workers. Inevitably people will come to resent and oppose others whose struggles over standards lead to plant shut-downs and benefits that accrue only to the strikers.

Among skilled jobs, sex separation has been and still is almost complete, despite the slight acceptance of women in some "nontraditional" jobs. Becoming a skilled worker was as unthinkable as flying to the moon. Still, because of society's persistent unwillingness to acquaint females with tools, mechanics, and industrial processes, to become a "woman craftsman" is, if anything, more remote than flying to the moon. I am repeatedly astonished in talking with young, active, liberated women who think, for instance, that plumbers only fix toilets, and who wants to do that?

My commitment to unionism undoubtedly made shop work far more stimulating than it otherwise would have been. I was not a cog or a robot. On the contrary, I had a purpose, a very human one at that. I wanted to function in the union. For many rank-and-file workers, unionism and the contest between workers and management, or between union factions, can, paradoxically, make many boring jobs endurable.

In my shop we had well-defined factions: the Blue Slate (the "left-wingers," the Thomas-Addis group) and the Green Slate (the Reuther group). The local balanced, during the years I was there, between the two, and then the Green Slate won out. When I was elected chief steward in trim, I became the first Green Slate steward ever elected in that department. I had a lot of help from the few women in the department and very little opposition from men.

My work as chief steward usually was absorbing and gratifying, but in fact I do not thrive on conflict, and the demands on my limited supply of combativeness were too great in the end. Also, I quickly sensed that workers and unionists were at least a generation away from accepting women as full partners. I felt as though I had walked in on a smoker, a male locker room, that I had opened a door that I, personally, would be better off shutting for the time being. I did just that. I returned to college and to academia, a somewhat more hospitable environment for women. Were I in the shop today, however, I think I'd give it a hell of a try. I know many women are now doing just that, including the woman local president whose remarks conclude this essay. "Right on," I say.

I have no nostalgia for the shop. I had a good job, by shop standards, and my workload was relatively light. But the environment was hard: dirty, grimy, noisy, uncomfortable, unattractive. These things probably count much more for women than for men, but they are vital parts of the work milieu for all of us. I loved the people, the variety of them, the toughness and honesty of them, their good humor and spontaneity. I very much like working with "blue-collar" men. The group bonding that occurs among them is an experience that is denied to most women. Men, factory men, have been much more a "collective" than women. But women are also acquiring some collective solidarity and, thankfully, we are moving at a pace that is swifter than "all due speed."

An outpouring of literature from the women's movement, long overdue, has informed us about career women—doctors, lawyers, professors, bosses—but we still know next to nothing about those eight in ten women who work but who have "jobs" rather than "careers." This includes women auto workers, the women in the shop and the offices, along with waitresses, shop clerks, dressmakers, and what have you.

About women auto workers, we don't even know such simple facts as how many women work in auto plants. The Census Bureau claims that in 1970 more than 128,068 women worked in the "motor vehicle and motor vehicle equipment" industry— 112,310 of them white, 13,749 Negro, and 2,009 of "Spanish heritage."[1] But is the "auto industry" synonymous with the "motor vehicle and motor vehicle equipment industry?" Who knows?

The Equal Employment Opportunities Commission (EEOC) claims that *in Michigan*, the auto capital, more than 340,000 people were employed in 1970 by "transportation equipment" employers, or at least by those reporting to EEOC. Of these, 37,381 were female and 64,308 were Negro (5,215 of them female).[2] Whether this gets us any closer to the facts is anybody's guess.

The EEOC figures do suggest that less than 10 percent of "transportation equipment" employees are women—a very small proportion for an industry in which, I believe, women could without much strain perform virtually all the jobs available.

The EEOC study also gives us some unique and hitherto unquantified insights into the maldistribution of the sexes in this industry, as shown in Table 1.

The old story, almost all the good jobs (officials, professionals, technicians, salesworkers, craftsmen) are held by white males— the jobs that pay off in money, prestige, power. The women and Negro males have what is left over. White women are almost evenly divided between clerical and operative jobs, and both Negro males and females are heavily concentrated among operatives. I should hasten to add that white males are also heavily into the operative jobs, creating an almost numerically balanced two-class system among white males: the unskilled workers on one hand and the upper echelons of skill and/or authority on the other. These are the sides that face each other over the bargaining table. Both women and Negro males hug the bottom of the office-shop hierarchies.

Table 1. Occupational Distribution in Michigan's Transportation Equipment Industry[3]

	Total females	Total males	Negro males	Negro females
Total white collar	15,412 (41.2)	77,683 (25.4)	2,678 (4.5)	788 (15.1)
Officials and managers	251 (.7)	29,713 (9.7)	942 (1.6)	1 (.0)
Professionals	511 (1.4)	22,400 (7.3)	261 (.4)	16 (.3)
Technicians	465 (1.2)	10,003 (3.3)	235 (.4)	20 (.4)
Salesworkers	36 (.1)	1,558 (.5)	14 (.0)	1 (.0)
Office and clerical	14,149 (37.9)	13,959 (4.6)	1,226 (2.1)	750 (14.4)
Total blue collar	20,216 (54.1)	218,460 (71.6)	53,668 (90.8)	4,186 (80.3)
Craftsmen	118 (.3)	45,214 (14.8)	2,256 (3.8)	1 (.0)
Operatives	18,715 (50.1)	160,775 (52.7)	47,807 (80.9)	4,052 (77.7)
Laborers	1,383 (3.7)	12,471 (4.1)	3,605 (6.1)	133 (2.6)
Service workers	1,753 (4.7)	9,168 (3.0)	2,747 (4.6)	241 (4.6)

Women auto workers need more facts. How many women in auto work? What is the female composition of each plant? How are the women distributed occupationally? What departments and classifications do they work in? What kinds of jobs are they excluded from? What are the skilled jobs and why aren't women doing them, or at least making a try? Are the seniority lists manipulated to keep women in place? Why can't some women, those who can and will, drive the trucks, operate the cranes, do the electrical work in the shop?

I am astonished to talk with active, healthy, liberated young women in auto shops who apparently still feel that women cannot operate machinery other than can openers or use tools other than butter knives. They are captives of habit. It's not that they reject the possibilities, it's that they simply don't think of them.

As for the UAW, my alma mater, union participation among women is high compared to other unions. The ideology is certainly democratic and egalitarian, and all the explicit policies and implicit feelings of the union's leadership favor full equity for women. But . . . in fact, all top elected policy positions in that union, with one exception, are held by males. The one exception is the designated female member of the executive board. She fills a spot created for women only. Contestants have no male opponents. This is all to the good since it is doubtful, as matters have stood, that any woman could win election to the board in an open contest. The woman board member is elected at large and has no regional constituency, as do other board members, most of whom are also regional directors.

Of the eight hundred or so "international representatives" on the union's top staff, only twenty are women, according to one recent count—about 2.5 percent of the total. These "reps" get out the vote for the regional directors.

Three women "reps" fill top appointed positions in the union. One is an assistant regional director. One is a department head—Women's Department. One is an assistant department head. None are administrative assistants to top officers.

Among secondary union leaders, action is more affirmative. Seventy-four women are local union presidents, or 5 percent of the total. Women are 7 percent of local vice presidents, 16 percent of financial secretaries, and 26 percent of recording secretaries. All in all, women occupy about 13.5 percent of these local leadership roles, which is proportional to their reported membership in the union. [4]

True, women are clustered in the traditional roles, especially that of recording secretary. But they also do quite well in the financial secretary category, a job of basic responsibility in the local. So basic are the collecting and dispensing of local funds that the financial secretary is the only full-time staff member in many locals.

These officers administer the local and seldom, except in the large plants, engage in collective bargaining. Shop committees do most of the bargaining. Only 85 women, or 4 percent of the total, are chief stewards, and 151 or 5 percent of the total are district committee people. Eighty-two women chair their local bargaining shop committees, and another 234 are members of those committees. Women are about 6 percent of all members of these committees—or about half of what an affirmative action goal might be.[5]

Women are better represented in other union functions, even key ones such as political action. Some 708 women are delegates to their county or area Community Action Program Council, or about 12 percent of the total. Political action comes easier to women because of the time element. The work can be arranged to suit family obligations and is familiar, like the neighborhood and church work many women do.

Add to these the women who are officers in local units (amalgamated locals or units of large plants) and members of local committees (recreation and conservation, constitution and by-laws, antidiscrimination, community services, education, consumer affairs, publicity, elections, retired members, apprenticeship, pension, supplementary unemployment benefits, women's councils)—and we come to a final grand total of more than 6,600 women who play active, significant roles in the UAW's secondary leadership. This is about 10 percent of the total. Not bad, considering the number of female union members.

A big barrier to women moving into top policy roles in the union is collective bargaining. The traditional role of women is in peripheral functions, especially health, education, welfare, and community work. Bargaining is thought to be man's work. While it is true that bargaining requires assertiveness, toughness, knowledge, shrewdness, and diplomacy, it is not true that men can claim to possess these qualities in greater abundance than women.

But even when women with negotiating experience are put on the national staff they are not assigned to the "service" staff that works on in-plant problems, but to the "special staffs" in education, political action, fair practices, and the like. Without staff experience in bargaining, women cannot compete for top policy roles in the union.

Again, time is a barrier. A woman cannot get up in the middle of a bargaining session and say, "Excuse me, fellows, I gotta pick up the kids." The show must go on, and the family must wait. I am reminded here of one of President Ford's would-be assassins, who reported that if the president's appearance had been delayed ten minutes more she would have had to go— to pick up her nine-year-old son at school. So it is with many women in the shop.

Another barrier to participation is the attitude of husbands. They want their wives home, not at meetings, or weekend conferences, or traveling around on union business. Going to work is one thing. There, at least he knows where she is and what she's doing. Of course, the shoe fits the other foot, too. Wives also keep many men from participating in the union. That is why the most active union people, male or female, have spouses who are also union people.

In the forties, the UAW set up a Women's Department to deal with the wartime influx of women into the shops. Before that, the only staff addressing itself to women was the Women's Auxiliary whose interest was chiefly in encouraging the wives of members to participate in service functions in the union.

Setting up the Women's Department was a controversial act. Some thought it would increase the segregation of women, limit rather than broaden the attention given them, and pacify their

27

demand for general representation. Supporters thought that women needed a staff to perform an advocate's role in the union. The women proved to be effective advocates. They were among the founders of NOW (the NAACP of the women's movement), and over the years they raised and won many shop and political issues for women.

UAW staff women were also among the chief movers in the formation of CLUW (Coalition of Labor Union Women), organized in 1974 to function outside union structures. The first president of CLUW was Olga Madar, formerly UAW vice president.

The UAW is still one of the few unions to have a women's department. Even now, the AFL-CIO has neither a women's representative nor a women's department.

Convention resolutions may not stir the blood, but they do stake out positions. These, from the women's rights resolution adopted at the 1974 UAW convention, indicate where UAW women would like to go: [6]

At the Workplace

Incorporate into our contracts clauses which will treat pregnancy in the same manner as any other disability.

Eliminate all discriminatory clauses in insurance plans which deny women, as a group, equal and fair treatment.

Eliminate restrictive seniority clauses, improper or unequal tests, both cultural and physical, wherever they may exist.

Implement the basic principle of equal pay for equal work in all newly organized plants and in those organized plants where contracts may fall short of this objective.

Police company hiring policies which curtail the employment of women.

Eliminate any restrictions pertaining to apprenticeable skilled trades classifications which deny women workers equal opportunity to train for such occupations.

Examine critically and constructively employer affirmative action programs, where required of government contractors, and insist that such programs be implemented.

Police contracts on a nondiscriminatory basis at all levels and advise women members of their rights and the procedures for filing complaints when discrimination is present.

Within the Union

Develop an affirmative action program to encourage participation by women in running for office.

Continue the current manpower training program providing the necessary vocational training to qualify women for apprenticeship opportunities.

The Women's and CAP Departments will jointly develop and implement a political education program to encourage and motivate union women to become candidates for elective and appointive public positions.

Urge local unions to include representatives of all minority groups, including women, on Fair Practices Committees, where this is not already being done.

Continue the program of regional and area women's conferences with emphasis on supplying women with information and skills to assist them in progressing on the job and in the union.

A Case in Point: Local Union President (female) [7]

I'm an Albanian and my husband is Italian-Sicilian. I guess the reason I became such a strong union person is that my father had to work all the time, morning, noon, and night to make a living for his family. It was the conditions that made my father a union person. After you slave all your life, and you never get anything, you realize that you need togetherness—union solidarity—to get anywhere.

Ever since I was a kid I used to take pity on the underdog. If there was a fight and they were picking on someone, I always got into it and tried to help the kid. Even now I say to myself, "I'm going to keep my mouth shut," and something happens and I'm in the middle of it.

I went to trade school and quit before I graduated. I got married at eighteen. When my kids were small I couldn't get involved with the union as much as I really wanted to. I helped organize, and when the union came in five years ago I ran for committeewoman and I lost. I ran again and won.

The pay had been good when the union came in, but people were concerned with conditions and the way they treated you, but they didn't stick together against the company. They were afraid to take a stand. More and more now they are beginning to stick up for themselves.

I made up my mind to run for president of the local. If I make up my mind I want something, I usually can get it. I ran against two men. I figured I really cared, and that this was what the people wanted. I was working on the night shift then, where there was mainly colored. It used to be that the colored voted for colored and the white for white. But they started coming to me for help. They thought I looked at the problem, not the person. The colored people backed me. That's the only way I could have got elected as committeewoman. So I crossed the race barrier, and then I had to cross the sex barrier. The committee backed a man.

In the few months I've been president, they've taken it out on me. Some people think that because I care and because I can fight, I can perform miracles. I can't. By myself I am nobody. I have to show the company that the people in the plant back me all the way. The company knows better than we do how split we have been.

Sometimes they speed the belt and people complain. We go there and time it and they slow it down. But then they speed it up again when they want to. Some of the girls are afraid to complain. Sometimes they load the line. They put two or three times as much material on it, and people can't keep up with it.

There is a problem of absenteeism with some people. They work us overtime so much that people have to take time off. If you work seven days, fifty-six hours, you're going to give out at some point. We're not machines. We wear out. We can't take that kind of overtime. When they ask us to work Sundays, we have to or we get disciplined. We take the cases up, and we win them, but it takes too long. They just harass us. When I worked nights, they used to keep women overtime until two in the morning. There is no public transportation at that hour. Yet they were disciplined if they didn't stay.

They can do what they want in enforcing the contract. But we can't make *them* abide by the contract. Contractually, they're supposed to respond to us in so many days, but if they don't, we can't do anything. But if our grievance is filed late after five days, they can dismiss it and call it untimely. I've waited as much as two months for an answer. You can't do anything. They don't have to pay a fine. You can't fire them.

Most people, if they realize you're trying to do something, will pitch in and help, or at least they'll say, "She's trying something." A few people like to gossip and criticize. That's not my bag. If I can't say something good about a person, I don't say anything. And I never was a nosy person, prying into people's personal business, so I never got into that much. I know somebody will object to whatever you do.

Men on my shift got behind me and pushed me to run for president more than the women did. But when I decided to run, the women supported me. Of course, some women said they thought a woman's place was in the home. I said to them, "Well, what are you doing in the plant?" I haven't learned to keep my mouth shut. The people who gave me the hardest time were the women who'd been there as long as I'd been there, who knew me real well. One of these girls was the biggest runaround in town, and she said my place was at home.

I think I would work even if I didn't have to. I don't think I'd be happy with a lot of leisure. When we were laid off, for many months, I got less done at home than I do when I'm working. I got in a rut. I thought I had plenty of time to do this or that, and I did nothing. The other way I do more. I keep on the move more. I see people more. It seems that the more I have to do, the better it is for me.

Some women say, "I don't think a woman can do the job as union president. It's too big a headache." I say, "Do you run your home? I run my home. It's a headache. You learn how to handle finances, get your kids ready for school, take care of their problems, sometimes your husband's problems. A woman has a bigger headache than a man, through their way of life, through the job they have to do at home. I think woman's role has been the biggest headache, so we're used to it."

It aggravates me when people say, "Why go to your union? The union doesn't do anything for you." I say, "How are we supposed to know what you want? You have to bring it to us or we can't help you." We all have to work on it. You, you, you, and me. We all are the union, together. I tell them, "We've got to forget that we're he-she, white-black. We got to make up our minds that we have to get together if we want to hold our own with the company."

I used to blow my top more when I was a committeewoman than I do now as president of the local. The company is used to me getting mad and hollering, which I haven't done since I've been president. I used to holler because I knew I didn't have the backing. Now what I say is the ground I can take. I've even gotten the foreman to blow his cool rather than me. I couldn't believe it. I stayed calm.

One time I was in negotiations and one of the supervisors said, "You're a hard man to deal with." Then he said, "I guess I shouldn't have said that." I didn't get insulted. I am a hard person to deal with. I knew what he meant.

I don't like it when things are too calm. I feel something's not right. They're hiding something or keeping it covered. I'd rather have something brought out and get it straightened out. Arguments don't bother me. I only get red in the face. Headaches I've always had. Arguments don't cause them. If I can get my points across, I forget my headache.

Some women, when they learn a job, don't want to be moved to another one. They're afraid to move. This has never been my problem. I'd like to try them all, learn them all. The company always knew when they wanted to try something new, they could always come to me. I see people working and I say, "If they can all do it, I can do it too." I stay in there. I don't let a job get the best of me. I have to master it.

The only thing that worried me about this job was chairing a meeting. Informally I can talk to anybody. I can go on and on. But when I get up there in front, that's something else. I've never made a public speech before, not that I can recall. You don't get much chance.

As I told the body at my first meeting, the only thing I didn't like about the job was this. But they told me I did very well. As I was chairing, I found I could answer the questions. As I do it more often, I won't mind it. I made up my mind that it was part of the job. I might be nervous the first few times, but I'd get over it.

Besides being president, I'm also chairman of the grievance committee. We have paid, full-time committeemen, one for every 250 employees. A lot of times when people come to me, they don't have a real grievance. Sometimes they've just gotten involved in fights with other people. We're trying to start a health and welfare committee to help people with personal problems.

If a woman wants to work, she has to keep her family together. She has to get her husband to agree, make him think it's his idea, that he's the important one, that all the time he's helping you. You have to learn how to manage your husband or get around him and make him feel he is the one who is helping you.

Notes

1. U.S. Bureau of Census, *Census of Population, 1970,* Vol. 1, *Characteristics of the Population,* pt. 1, U.S. Summary, section 2, Table 236, Detailed Industry of Employed Persons by Race and Sex, p. 801.
2. 1970 Equal Employment Opportunities Report, Vol. 1, *Job Patterns for Minorities and Women in Private Industry* (Washington, D.C.: U.S. Government Printing Office, 1972).
3. Ibid.
4. Research Department, UAW, "UAW Survey of Women 1973" (Detroit: UAW, 1973), mimeo.
5. Ibid.
6. "Resolution on Women's Rights," *Proceedings at the 24th Constitutional Convention UAW,* Los Angeles, Calif., June 2–6, 1974, p. 339.
7. Personal interview with local union president, December 5, 1974.

3

The Skilled Trades: Reflections

Bill Goode

Prior to the organization of industrial unions, the skilled workers in America were truly an "aristocracy of labor." Commanding higher wages and a near monopoly of a specific skill, they worked in isolation from the rest of the American work force. They were predominantly building tradesmen or in craft unions such as the Railroad Engineers.

The Congress of Industrial Organizations (CIO) organized the skilled workers in the auto shops for the first time. Disdained by the old AFL, they had never experienced the exclusiveness of their counterparts on the "outside." As industrial workers they were organized into the same union as production workers. Consequently, the skilled auto worker looked both ways, "outside" to his peers in the craft unions and "inside" to his fellow unionists in the UAW.

Almost all auto workers, if given a chance, would exchange places with the skilled tradesmen in their shop. The pay is better and perhaps because of that the status is higher. Skilled workers are more apt to get precious overtime. But the most envied aspect of skilled work is its apparent freedom. Nothing compares with the relentless tedium of a moving line or the demands of an hourly production quota.

To the production worker, the skilled tradesman seems singularly free of the urgency of work. He seems only to walk around the plant all day, perhaps carrying some tools, perhaps pushing his wagon of tools and fittings. (I remember when I became an apprentice feeling that that those damned draftsmen and engineers never seemed to be busy.)

Consequently, in the Big Three shops, 15 percent of the work force (skilled) are envied for their freedom, their pay, and their perceived better working conditions.[1] In September 1975, a major assembler in the auto plants made about $5.25 an hour, plus an 84¢ cost-of-living float, for a total of $6.19 an hour. They also have the finest fringe benefits in industry, medical and dental coverage, a retirement plan, and life insurance.[2]

The skilled worker's pay varied by classification. An electrician made, with the cost-of-living allowance, about $7.56 an hour. A toolmaker was paid 10¢ an hour more. A millwright made about $7.32 an hour.[3] The differential of a dollar to a dollar and a half an hour is a source of irritation to the unskilled worker. Every negotiation is marked by low-level rumbling about this differential, and occasionally it erupts into a major internecine battle within the union.

It should be emphasized that while this division along skill lines is a problem for the union, all attempts to organize the skilled workers into a separate union have been complete failures. Industrial unionism is the overwhelming choice of both production and skilled workers in the auto industry.

One accommodation that the UAW had to make was to grant the skilled trades the right to separate ratification of the contracts. This has been criticized by some as a step backward from the original purity of industrial unionism. On the other hand, this move permitted the skilled worker a stronger sense of identity and recognition of his own very real problems.

While the production worker looks to the skilled worker, the skilled worker is looking outside at his peers in the building trades making approximately $12.00 an hour.[4]

One aspect of skilled work that production workers do not usually experience is dirt. With the exception of some skilled jobs (gauge inspectors, for example) skilled work is filthy. The maintenance and construction crews work in places that are usually not cleaned in most shops, underground, under floors, in the air around pipes and conduit that may not have been touched in years. Oil is ubiquitous. Solvent cleaners and harsh soaps are used to clean exposed parts of the body. Compressed air is used to get dirt out of coveralls. Even the toolmakers have to handle materials covered with oil. The skilled worker carries the marks of his trade under his fingernails and in the creases of his hands.

Looking the other way, the skilled auto worker sees the big wages of his peers on the outside, but he doesn't see the seasonal nature of that work, the fact that it is most often not in a closed building, that the work is harder because there are no lulls caused by the nature of servicing a production facility.

Next to overtime grievances, the most vexing problem for a skilled committeeman or steward was outside contracting of work within a plant. It meant that every time a rigging company came into our shop to move a group of machines our crew lost that work and the probability of overtime. But, more important, it was a terrible blow to the pride of the regular worker. There is probably a sound economic reason for the contracts, having to do with fringe benefits for new workers if the job was too large for the existing crew, just as there probably is justification for forcing men to work overtime instead of putting on more men or another shift. But to the workers these decisions are an affront, a slur on their skills, "and besides they pay them more!" The rage expressed over contracting of work is monumental. In almost every case adequate men and equipment existed to cover the job. Certainly a capricious management was responsible for much of this activity. Management discussions with the union are necessary prior to letting an outside contract, but discussions with the workers would also prove of value. There never has been a job, regardless of the skill of engineering, that workers have not been able to improve upon and shorten the operating time.

The movement between the "outside" and "inside" workers was minimal. Every once in a while, outside journeymen, perhaps tired of the booming tradition, or the unsettled nature of work, or simply because of a layoff, would come into the shops. They never left. All of the enticements of outside work, high wages and all, could not get them to return. The shops represented a very real security. Journeymen in auto shops often have ten to forty years of seniority in one place; outside skilled men brag about working a year and a half on one location.

Occasionally, there would be movement from inside to outside. One electrician in our gang was offered a job on the outside working on permit. (Work permits are granted by the craft union to some journeymen when the job market is good, but the permit workers seldom get a regular journeyman's card regardless of how long the job lasts.) He was also given a conditional promise that a card would be wangled for him in a few months (or years). This was risky and he knew it, but his ambition was to have a shop of his own.

Despite the apparent envy of the skilled men in the captive shops of their counterparts on the outside, the electrician anguished for days over the decision. It meant giving up his seniority which would have assured him of a steady job; it meant risk, the outcome of which he could not possibly foresee. He took the job, and in the casual nature of relationships in a large industrial city we never heard of him again. At least, we know he did not subsequently apply for a job at our plant.

Getting out of the shops grinds less on the skilled group than it does on production workers, but it does exist. Only one skilled trades committeeman quit in a decade at Ford Highland Park. His family was involved in a prosperous retail outlet, and he first took a leave for several months. Then he returned for a like period. Finally he left to join the family business. Part of the trouble is the jealously guarded seniority list. There are provisions in the contract for union leaves and personal leaves, but workers do not accept the idea that seniority of someone who is outside gainfully employed should remain intact.

Education was recognized as a way to escape from the shops, and education was prized even if it did not achieve this end. An articulate, knowledgeable worker is respected. During the Korean War a new employee in his early forties made a literate, effective speech at a local meeting. Anticipating the other members, he asked rhetorically, "You are probably thinking, what's he doing working in a factory?" He was right; that was exactly the question in many minds. Some grumbled that the Communist party probably planted him. Education was admired and respected, but there was also considerable ambivalence about the literate folk.

On Monday morning I occasionally took a section of the *New York Times* into work to read at lunch. As I was the only apprentice and the youngest man in the gang, this action gave rise to some good-natured raillery. "Hey, Goode, what kind of communist literature you bringing in now?"

One of the best mechanics and most respected fitters in the gang made a public defense of my reading habits. He told me later in private: "Don't let them kid you. I always read the financial pages of the *Times*. My girl friend lived in Detroit and I came here to get married, never expecting to stay thirty-five years. But I got out of World War I, made a bad investment of my money and here I am."

"What did you invest in, Jimmy?"

"Czarist rubles," was the reply.

The tradition of the old mechanic, self-taught, job-trained, is disappearing, replaced by a system of apprenticeships. Young men are now given a grounding in mathematics, physics, and theory of the trade. Reactions vary. Some apprentices "took low" and dutifully went to the crib to get a left-handed monkey wrench or went on other fool's errands because it was expected of them and they played their role. Others rebelled at the status of the older men and fought back. One apprentice, not so innocently, asked the only master plumber in the gang how he could possibly consider himself a master without ever having taken a course in trigonometry. That bit of baiting caused an immediate explosion. The old mechanic in a few thousand well-chosen words told the "young punk" where he could shove his trigonometry.

Comparable to the permit worker on the outside are the upgraders or Employees in Training (EIT). When there is a major move or model change, production workers with some experience are brought into the skilled trades to supply the necessary manpower. They stay as long as the work lasts and then go back to their old jobs. Their presence often causes uneasiness. Skilled workers obviously want the production worker to get a break, but they also jealously guard their craft and carefully watch the seniority list to see that their positions are maintained.

The life of an assembler has been recorded by many authors, but there have been few observers of the skilled trades in auto plants. Given all of the material on the "iron horse" of the assembly line, little has been written on the level of the interaction among workers. Assemblers, the intrinsic nature of the job apart, simply have more fun. There is a spontaneity about the play on a line that is unmatched by skilled work.

An assembly line always has artifacts for involved horseplay: tubing, metal washers, bolts, empty kegs, all provide the materials for elaborate gags. This play is largely slapstick, never subtle, and often with more than a touch of malice. A handful of washers on a steel floor will tip over a cart that a worker sits on to wheel himself under a car body. Tubing and cold water provide great, if not delicate, possibilities for humor.

There are always "cony catchers" on the line, those verbal con men who can convince the village idiot that there are oil deposits under his house lot and that people are out to steal it. Or the deflator tells the macho bear-killer that his prize must have been about the size of a small dog. "Did the cub come up and lick your hand before you shot it?" It is hard to tell whether the fool is an innocent of wit as it seemed or was just playing a role because it helped kill time in a pleasant way.

For the auto worker, particularly the skilled worker, killing time was a real problem. Stories about doubling up on a moving line always leave out something. There is an implication that two workers can handle each other's jobs, one doing two jobs, while the other loafs. Four hours' work, eight hours' pay. There is no assembly line in any auto plant where it is possible to double up for more than a few minutes at a time. The extra burst of energy needed to do this is sometimes invigorating for a short period but it is killing over a long period.

But skilled work is spasmodic. There is a division between the maintenance and construction crew (electricians, pipefitters, millwrights, riggers, the building trades) and the tool and die section (toolmakers, machine hands, and machine repairmen). The work flow for the latter tends to be more regular, work for the former depends on breakdowns or need for new installations of air lines or water, installing new machinery, or changing lines.

Maintenance work is hard, physically exhausting and very often demanding great strength. Pipefitters in self-denigration refer to the necessary attributes of their trade as "a strong back and a weak mind." The tool and die section is always considered the prestigious part of skilled work.

A break from hard work would seem to be a treat, but most workers are so defensive about loafing that they create elaborate rationales excusing the lack of work for which they have no responsibility or control. The commonest excuse is: "When I'm sitting on my ass the company is making money, when I have to work it means something is broken down and the company is losing money."

The vast majority of skilled workers believe in hard work and take pride in it. The "good mechanic" has a special status in the shops, however bad-natured or even antiunion he may be. His opposite, the "shoemaker" or less-talented worker, is given short shrift. But the most despised worker is the lazy one. Stewards or committeemen are often accused of being elected to office because no one could get any work out of them.

Much of the attitude about work evinced by older workers is partly a result of the old, brutal, preunion days in the shops. A fitter one time told me never to be caught sitting down. If you had no job at the time, stand at your bench with a piece of wire in your hand so you could always say that you were making a pipe hanger if you were asked.

There is general disapproval, mostly among supervisors, at the sight of any worker idling. The sight of a sitting tradesman can produce great anxiety in a boss, particularly a superintendent or general foreman. In reality, the work flow is not evenly distributed in time and workers may not have an assignment on occasion. Consequently the foreman is placed in the position of creating makework or telling the crew to hide. To the workers this is sanctioned loafing time. The foreman usually knew where his men were hiding or told them to come back in an hour. A foreman who had worked for a long time with a crew knew their hiding places and probably had shared them when he was in overalls.

The subterfuges extended even when working. One of the most decent human beings I have ever known was a great ex-pug (Ford's was full of them) who had fought in Harry Greb's stable. We were working off of the board one day, doing maintenance jobs as things broke down. We had a fairly busy day and every time a job came up he told me to get the tools and a plunger. After several jobs we had a call to fix a drinking fountain. The orders were the same, "get the plunger." I said, "Bricky, what do we need a plunger for to repair a water fountain?" He looked at me with great scorn. "When are you going to grow up? Don't you know that nobody ever asks a pipefitter where he's going if he has a plunger over his shoulder?" This is the way apprentices learn.

While skilled workers dislike a lazy worker, they do enjoy a monumental rip-off of the company. There is usually a lull in work just prior to a model changeover. Major changes are in the offing and things are generally in good shape. Supervision tends to get sloppy, and the atmosphere is relaxed and easygoing. Two millwrights had found an old time clock and, being good mechanics, they got it into working order. For a month they came in late and left early, setting the clock to the time they wanted, punching their time cards and leaving them in the rack. This required considerable ingenuity because they had to know when the timekeeper was going to pick up their cards. The rest of the crew admired their audacity because they beat the company at its own game. They used the resented clock, the worst of the surveillance mechanisms, to defeat the company.

There was the usual amount of drinking during the work day, usually at lunchtime. Seldom did workers bring a bottle on the job. Because of the different shifts in a large plant, workers streamed in and out constantly. If a crew had a few beers at lunch they may have decided to extend their thirty-minute lunch to an hour. When they got caught, the committeeman had to do a "knee pad job," that is, try to wheedle the supervisor or labor relations man into forgiving the offense without a penalty. These negotiations were usually cajolery, the union pleading non compos mentis or chronic alcoholism as a defense. These minor infractions resulted in a network of mutual obligation and reciprocity between the union and management. It takes considerable skill to operate in this setting without one party completely dominating the other. This entirely justified trading off kept the already crowded grievance procedure relatively free of minor cases.

Working with a drunk partner is at best a terrible inconvenience and at worst very dangerous. If you are working on the ground, the rhythm of work is disturbed. Ordinary mechanical operations become matters of great concentration for the drinker and great exasperation for his partner. If you are working in the air the problem is critical. A wrench dropped from even ten feet can fracture a skull. Occasionally, workers will refuse to work with someone who has been drinking. A crane operator, lifting heavy loads in a bay that may be two to six floors high, is a positive menace. Most new plants are one-floor structures, but older plants were built up rather than out.

Drinking and loafing are both ways of killing time. The point was just to make it to three-thirty, the end of the shift. Even if it were possible to find a hole to sleep in, rest was not the point, only killing time. Work discipline was maintained by external authority for some, a hectoring foreman. For some, the discipline was internalized, almost a compulsion to keep busy and do your job. For a small percentage (far too few) the motivation was pleasure, the sheer joy of working at a job they genuinely liked.

The ambivalence toward work is best illustrated by the attitude toward those elected to union office. If someone was defeated in an election, he "went back to work." Union activity is not considered work. Work is by nature arduous and onerous. If it is not hard and dirty, it's not work. Highland Park, Michigan, an enclave inside Detroit, was for years a center of the Finnish community. Many Finns held a strong evangelical, low-church religious belief. It was interesting to hear two old friends raised in the same neighborhood, both intensely religious, discuss the nature of work. One day at lunch, someone asked whether there would be work in heaven. Their answers were instantaneous and diametrically opposed. One maintained that work was punishment for the sin of Adam and Eve and that, of course, there would be no work in heaven. The other asserted with equal vehemence that work was fulfillment, that it was man's nature to work, and there would certainly be work in heaven. The argument raged all lunch hour, and it was probably one of the most interesting debates I have heard on the nature of work, certainly surpassing much of the disputation that occurs in sociological circles.

The racial harmony in our gang in the old days was unbelievable compared to today's relationships. It was an artificial situation, a compound of company paternalism and a high seniority group with long experience working together. Old man Ford always had a numerus clausus for blacks in his plants. Our skilled group was 10 percent black, which about reflected the general population figures but did not reflect the population of Detroit.

Fifteen years after the event, white tradesmen recalled with indignation a white brother who caviled at contributing money for a watch traditionally given to workers going into the army during World War II because the worker was black. There was just something too damned unfair about it that these workers resented his blatant bigotry. On one occasion hundreds of workers stormed over to the union hall on a wildcat strike when it was thought that one of the highest seniority blacks was being denied his rights on shift preference.

Of equal interest would be to watch the reaction of skilled workers as women first invade the nonapprenticeable trades, tool grinding and others, and eventually reach into the construction trades. That would be a dandy to see.

The skilled trades in the auto industry are harassed by the same problems facing all workers, layoffs, racial friction, and the growing demands of women for entrance into this previously exclusively male group. But they have their particular problems also. A new technology will create new trades, new skills that will challenge the old rankings.

Bull work is disappearing from the shops, and automation will continue to decrease the difference between production and skilled work. Paradoxically, all work will become more sophisticated, presumably to disappear into a monitoring function. The number of auto workers will not increase at the same rate as the work force. There will be less looking to the outside as a reference group to gauge their success and a greater disposition to accommodate to the rising skill level of all work.

But the line will be with us for a while and the distinction between production worker and skilled worker will continue. While there may be no work in heaven, there will be plenty of it on earth, and the skilled worker has much the better of it. Uneasy, threatened, and yet proud of his work, the tradesman represents a great tradition in American working-class life.

As a footnote, it is interesting that the five of us writing these papers all concluded that the days in the auto shops were major influences in our lives. For four of us it was an overwhelming one. Personally, I dream still about shops, very often disquieting dreams. That ten years working on production and as a pipefitter and union committeeman was the most productive education I have ever received. The local union politics could be savage, but the UAW is a yeasty, feisty union composed of some of the greatest men and women I have ever met. Without them we would all be much diminished.

Notes

1. The number of skilled tradesmen in the UAW is hard to estimate because of the variety of contracts and different methods of classification. The UAW Skilled Trades Department estimates that 15 percent of the Big Three are skilled.

2. General Motors press release, September 16, 1975.

3. UAW Research Department data, from personal interview, October 1, 1975.

4. Ibid.

4

Alienation and Dehumanization?

Robert Reiff

A long time ago I had occasion as a psychologist to work with a group of seriously mentally and physically handicapped children. I remember the first few days of my contact with them. I experienced a kind of "humanitarian shock." I could see nothing but their handicaps, and I felt alienated from them, as though these "unfortunate" children were something less than human. As I continued to work with them I found their personalities emerging, and their handicaps almost seemed to disappear in my perception of them. I think that something of the same process occurs when social scientists look at production workers. They do not see them as human beings, but as mechanized robots, and project their own feelings of alienation on them. The point of all this is that my experience working in an auto plant has convinced me that alienation of workers as a personality characteristic is in the eyes of the social science beholder.

The general claims of alienation and dehumanization are exaggerated and misleading. The concept of alienation often differs depending on which branch of social science the observer identifies with. Clinical psychologists, for example, speak of alienation as a personality variable, usually an intrapsychic one. To some social psychologists alienation is an organizational variable, while to others it is a personality variable resulting from the nature of the interaction between the person and the work environment. Sociologists also think of alienation as a personality variable, but they attribute it to the social organization of the production process. As such they consider it to be a social phenomenon shaping the behavior of all who are engaged in the production process. It is interesting that almost all social scientists, no matter which concept they hold, acknowledge Marx as the origin of their beliefs.

Marx's assumptions about alienation are based on the conflict between the private ownership of the means and products of production and the producers of the products, that is, the workers. He uses the term "alienation" to describe the factory workers' relationship to the raw material, the process or means, and the finished product, none of which the worker has any formal or legal control over. Alienation, therefore, in the Marxian sense, is not a personality characteristic but a descriptive term to indicate the social and economic relationship between the workers as producers and the product as well as the means of production. If it is a characteristic at all it is of the social structure of production rather than of personality. [1]

I have found that the degree of alienation as a personality characteristic in production workers, or the extent of it among them, is no greater than exists among plant managers and owners of the means of production. As a psychologist who has had a great deal of contact with disturbed and alienated people, I have found there is little or no relationship between alienation as a personality characteristic and the ownership or control of the means of production. If alienation is a personality characteristic, it is more likely to be related to such social structural characteristics as the institutional orders of the family, child-rearing practices, the educational system, and religious and ethical practices. In many cases the work situation provided a compensatory milieu for whatever alienating effects were experienced elsewhere.

My experience in an auto plant has been that workers show a great deal of initiative in developing ways to get satisfaction out of the work *situation* rather than the product itself. The means of production and the product are transformed by workers into meaningful and satisfying *situations*, from which they find ways of establishing their own identities. The production worker is almost always part of a group. There are many opportunities for social relationships in the work situation, and these are often crucial in providing satisfaction. I knew one worker whose major satisfaction from work was that he was almost always the first one to show up in the morning. Another drew satisfaction because he was famous for eating more lunch than anyone else in the plant. Others had more profound satisfactions and identities as informal leaders, outspoken critics, lucky gamblers, and so on. One could almost develop a typology of satisfactions and identities that provide satisfaction (or dissatisfaction) within the work situation.

Perhaps not typical, but not uncommon, was Mike. In addition to his work on the production line Mike was a union counselor. He devoted a great deal of his time on the job and after working hours to providing an invaluable service to the other workers. Mike's function as a union counselor was to help the members receive the full benefits to which they were entitled from the union and from public and community service organizations and agencies. Frequently a union member failed to get these benefits because he did not know what was available and how to get it. Mike's function was not just educational. He informed the members of their privileges and assisted those who needed help by interpreting the rules, regulations, and laws to them. But he also acted as the member's representative, attempting to break through unnecessary delay, using the power of the union as a lever if needed. Mike was the opposite of an alienated man, and there were hundreds of union counselors like him in the UAW.

Years later, when I had become a professional, Frank Riessman and I published a monograph on the indigenous nonprofessional which played an important part in starting and developing the growth of the paraprofessional movement in this country. I had Mike in mind as the prototype for the concept of the paraprofessional.[2]

Of course, social structure plays a role in shaping human behavior. But the product and the means of production are not the only shaping factors of the social structure of production.

Other characteristics are: it provides a means of making a living for oneself and one's family; it provides a milieu for inter-personal relationships; it provides a context for social activities and the like.

Some social scientists are fond of speaking about the dehumanization that takes place in workers as a result of the production process, by which they mean that production workers feel like robots, or interchangeable, mechanical parts that have no choice but to obey mechanical laws. The concept implies blind obedience, apathy, a feeling of complete loss of control over one's actions and options. I am sure that some emotionally or psychologically disturbed workers feel that way, but by no means does this describe any significant number of production workers. On the contrary, they feel angry at being exploited, re-sentful at being mistreated, frustrated at the limited control they do have. It is because they feel *human* that they have these feelings.

The term "dehumanization" has another meaning as the process in which social structures compel people to act toward other people as though they were less than human. On rare occasions, in exceptional circumstances, I have seen production workers temporarily act this way. On the other hand, such be-havior is a daily occurrence for industrialists, bankers, bosses, bureaucrats, politicians, and in particular workers in social ser-vice agencies. The social structure of social service agencies, particularly public ones, seems to produce dehumanized be-havior by its workers toward others. It would be interesting to study what conditions in production work and social service work account for this difference. In any case, the issue in "de-humanization" is not what produces these feelings but what produces dehumanized behavior toward others.

What effects does the social structure in which the production line is the organizing feature have on the internal and external social behavior of production workers? I could not presume to give a methodological answer to such a complicated yet signifi-cant question. However, my experience and observations as a production worker and my subsequent professional training and experience have led me to the following analysis.

It has been said that man's work is his contact with reality. In a sense his work defines reality for him, and his definition of reality helps to determine how he copes, defends, and adapts. In short, his relationship to work plays a part in shaping his character and personality. The social reality of a production worker is as different from the social reality of a preindustrial worker as it is from that of a middle-class intellectual. Though we often think and act as though there is a unitary social reality of society, there is, in fact, a composite of different social realities. I think we can learn something from a comparison of the structural characteristics of the preindustrial world of work as performed by the artisan with the structural characteristics of the industrial world of work as performed by the production line worker.

The world of work as performed by the artisan was organized by a fundamental focus on quality. The fundamental task of an artisan was to create a product out of his own personal manipulation of materials. He selected the materials and worked them into the finished product. He was free to compose the product from his own aesthetic judgment and a knowledge of his own individual resources and skills as well as the materials he used. He was, in fact, a composer. As such, his sense of creativity was developed with its concomitant effect on his self-image and his relationship to the world of people and objects. The palpable characteristics of materials, goods, and objects were of deep and immediate concern to him. His relationship to them was intimate and personal. He relied not only on his distal receptors but on his promixal as well. His sense of touch, his proprioceptive and kinesthetic responses were crucial to his understanding of the characteristics of materials and objects. The product he made was an immediate and direct reflection of his total self, his internal and external physical as well as his aesthetic and intellectual component.

The artisan was a man of self-discipline. He set his own standards of excellence and prospered or perished by them. He created his own workplace, which was usually solitary. He was not dependent on the work of others and therefore was not group-minded except perhaps in a feeling of affinity with those who produced similar products. He was not interchangeable or replaceable by any other person. The work he performed represented a challenge with a relative absence of threat from the work itself. Of course, other social, political, and economic factors over which he had no control made *life* threatening or dangerous, but in his relations to the product his control was absolute and unchallengeable.

In contrast, the world of work as performed by the production worker is organized by a fundamental focus on quantity. The worker on the production line has no control over the composition or quality of the product. The design of the product, the inherent quality of the materials, the process of composing or assembling it are all predetermined. Quantity alone is supposed to organize his energies. The skill of a line worker depends on such things as his reaction time, his spatial orientation, his ability to coordinate and control the movements of his body. There is very little room for aesthetic judgment or for composition. His skill depends on coordinated and controlled repetitive movements, sometimes with a delicate sensitivity to time or spatial orientation. Since he has no part in the design of the product his self-value or self-esteem is not derived from the product. Consequently, it is not in the work itself but in the workplace that he finds the satisfactions he needs.

The production worker is subject to an imposed discipline by rules and regulations and by the nature of the work. He must coordinate his work with those on the line who work before him and those who work after him. Production line work by its very nature cannot be solitary. The line worker therefore is compelled to be group-minded and interpersonally active.

The determination of the precise task that most workers perform lies in chiefly local, temporary, and fortuitous circumstances. He can easily be replaced or interchanged.

These conditions add up to considerable and realistic threat as well as posing the question of the degree of control the production line and the company have over him. Where unions are part of the structure they play an important role in altering the manner and degree to which this is accomplished.

The conventional production line at the present time requires men to operate it. Without manpower the production line is useless. The present organization of production makes it possible for those working on the line to exercise some degree of control. It is a basis for economic power and political clout through which the worker can express and fight for his needs and desires. That was and still is the role the UAW plays in the life of the line worker.

Notes

1. Karl Marx, "Alienated Labor," in Eric and Mary Josephson eds. *Man Alone* (New York: Dell, 1962), pp. 93–105.
2. Robert Reiff and Frank Reissman, "The Indigenous Nonprofessional Community," *Mental Health Journal,* 1 (1966).

5

Black Workers: Double Discontents

B. J. Widick

Black workers, men and women, in the auto industry have seldom been given proper attention in the vast array of articles and studies about work in this highly visible industry.

In most of the studies about work and its discontents in the auto industry there has been a basic hypothesis which is open to question—the assumption that a composite model, statistical or otherwise, may be drawn of the "typical" or "average" auto worker. A similar assumption has been employed in most studies about the "typical" American worker—the machinist in Dayton, Ohio. No one has demonstrated how the factor of race can be factored into the equation.

The significant differences, in spite of some similarities, between the lot of the black workers and that of white workers have been obscured or ignored in the statistical generalizations in many surveys. The disadvantage of race, when your color is black, and the handicap of late entry into the industrial work force by blacks are sources of special discontent, as the record of black struggles in the auto industry testifies.

The 1974-75 recession, with close to 40 percent of the auto industry blue-collar work force unemployed at times, served as a reminder that the basic source of dissatisfaction among those workers is not so much job alienation, as many critics contend, as it is alienation from the job, that is, unemployment. As the last to be hired and the first to be fired, under the rules of the seniority system operating in the contracts between the auto workers' union and the industry, black workers always have the highest rate of unemployment in any production cutbacks and are the most sensitive to the issue of job security. What preys on their minds is job loss—always an imminent danger.

Of course, until World War II, the issues of work dissatisfaction bypassed the black community in auto centers. Black efforts concentrated on trying to obtain a foothold in the industrial complex—notably in the auto industry—with very little success. Job alienation was a concept as unknown to the black as to the peasant who left Europe and came into our industrial vortex. For blacks—as against the peasant and Southern workers who were induced into the auto plants—the burning issue was discrimination in hiring. The nearly total exclusion of black workers from the auto plants may be seen in the 1941 figures. Only in the Ford Motor Company were there a significant number of black workers, about 11,000, or 10 percent of the work force. But most of them were restricted to dirty foundry work, general labor, and janitorial assignments. In the spring of 1941, Chrysler hired 1,850 blacks, which amounted to 2.5 percent of its work force in the Detroit area. About 1,400 of these were in the Dodge motor division, again mainly in the foundries. A large Packard plant had about 400 black workers, while at the Hudson factories there were 225 blacks out of a total 12,000 employees; Murray Body Corporation had about 315 black workers—about 5 percent of its total work force. Out of 22,000 employees at Briggs Manufacturing Company, about 7 percent were blacks. They were used mainly in the paint shops or as handlers of labor materials. [1]

That was the world of Jim Crow—the auto industry was a mirror of American society. In the book *The UAW and Walter Reuther*, management attitudes were expressed in an interview given prior to World War II. It was similar to views frequently heard in our early arguments about black employment in the plant. The interviewer wrote: "I asked if Negroes were not employed anywhere in the plant. He said, 'Yes, some jobs white folks will not do; so they have to take niggers in, particularly in duce work, spraying paint on car bodies. This soon kills a white man.' I inquired if it never killed Negroes. 'Oh yes,' he replied, 'It shortens their lives, it cuts them down but they're just niggers.''' [2] It took over five years in plant negotiations with foremen and superintendents for them to grasp the idea that I was hostile to their language and that I really believed in UAW policy of equal job opportunities. Most active UAW stewards who carried out union policy had similar experiences. Walter Reuther's eloquence on the subject was a morale booster for the UAW activists, black and white, during the postwar period. Before that, it was tough.

As Irving Howe and I wrote in that book,

> With the outbreak of the war in 1941, a new crisis in race relations arose in the auto plants. A few of the major causes may be briefly noted:
>
> (1) The influx of new Southern white workers brought into the union thousands of men who had not gone through strike experience at the side of the Negroes and who knew nothing of the tradition of tolerance that had been slowly developed in the union.
>
> (2) The Detroit housing crisis aggravated tensions between Negro and white.
>
> (3) The exclusion of Negroes from auto plants at a time when government officials were bemoaning a manpower shortage aroused enormous resentment among Negroes.
>
> (4) President Roosevelt's Executive Order 8802, establishing a committee for fair-employment practices and prohibiting discrimination in war industries was hailed by Negroes. But when it was largely ignored by industry and loosely enforced by the government, Negro resentment against wartime Jim Crow was aggravated still further. [3]

Wildcat strikes against hiring Negroes were broken by an aggressive UAW leadership; management attitudes shifted under government pressure, and perhaps most important of all, labor market shortages were so great that only blacks and women could fill the manpower needs. A. Phillip Randolph's threat of a march on Washington in protest over hiring discrimination had intense support in the Detroit black community. Even the bloody antiblack race riot failed to halt the slow progress of black employment which reached seventy-five thousand men and women in the war plants. Chrysler, for example, went from zero black women to about five thousand in April 1945. [4]

During the painful transition from war to peacetime production, mass layoffs of blacks (and whites also) occurred, and when blacks were rehired they were channeled back into the traditional patterns of dirty and menial jobs. But there was an important difference. Under the UAW-auto industry contracts, the blacks had accumulated seniority rights. Women's rights were flagrantly violated until the UAW, on perfectly sound legal grounds under the contracts, won a major arbitration decision at the Dodge truck plant involving the discriminatory layoff of thirty-one black women. This was a significant precedent.

But the road to equality on the job and promotion or transfer to other departments was rough. As I wrote elsewhere,

> Nor did the numerous wildcat strikes succeed in stopping the promotion or the introduction of black workers into all jobs and areas within the plants—the exception being the skilled trades, where no real progress in breaking down discrimination was made for twenty years. . . .
>
> Under UAW pressure, the auto companies finally began to penalize wildcat strikers who refused to work with Negroes, but in some cases it wasn't easy, as lower echelon management often shared the workers' antiblack feelings.
>
> A typical situation occurred in a metal shop employing 2,000 men, half of whom were Southern workers, the rest Polish or Italian. Under the union contract, the expansion of seniority rights gave Negroes a chance to apply for metal finishing work, attractive because it paid 15 cents an hour more than assembly jobs. The whites refused to break in the Negroes, and walked out. In a raucous union meeting the issue was resolved when the wildcatters were threatened with discharge unless they returned to work.
>
> In another instance, union officials insisted on a firm commitment from the company that it would fire ringleaders of any anti-Negro walkout. This prevented a work stoppage since the potential wildcatters knew they would lose their jobs permanently. It didn't lessen their prejudice but it did establish job rights for many Negroes. [5]

As black employment increased in the postwar period, the white UAW activists, including the team working with me on this project, were able to withstand the epithet "nigger-lover" in local union elections. The political power generally of blacks in the UAW began to increase, encouraged by the stance of the international union, notably Walter Reuther. And the term "nigger" began to disappear in the shops as blacks asserted themselves, sometimes physically. In my plant, the most popular chief steward on the once all-white assembly line was Otis Pickett, a black, self-educated time-study expert, and a good bargainer. He was so effective that his opposition was always minimal. Later he became night plant superintendent, a far cry from the days when management thought a black request for black foremen was absurd.

In contrast to white workers, black auto workers were constantly harassed in seeking the use of public facilities, eating in restaurants, in their treatment by police, and in their attempts to break out of the ghetto housing. There always seemed to be a white mob somewhere, picketing a new black neighbor. Both in and out of the plants, life had a special hard quality for blacks. And then there was always the specter of unemployment. As new hires in the postwar period, blacks tended to be the first out on the street. In 1945-46, it was the impact of reconversion. Then the 1949-50, the 1953-54, the 1958-59, and worst of all, the 1974-75 recessions. Black unemployment was always at least double white unemployment.

As for promotion or entry into the world of the aristocracy of labor, the skilled trades, blacks were able to make only token progress, in spite of various campaigns or commitments by Walter Reuther and the UAW. The Civil Rights Commission was given these figures by two black labor leaders, Horace Sheffield and Robert Battle III, of the UAW. The 1960 figures for black workers were: tool and die makers, 159 or 7/10 of 1 percent; structural steelworkers, 26 or 1/2 of 1 percent; printing craftsmen, 15 or 9/10 of 1 percent; carpenters, 360 or 2/10 of 1 percent; electricians, 163 or 2.1 percent; and machinists or job setters, 900 or 5.2 percent—these were industrywide figures. In the Detroit area, Chrysler had 24 black workers in skilled trades out of 7,425 workers; General motors listed 67 skilled black workers out of a total of 11,125, and Ford had 250 skilled black workers out of 7,000.[6]

Like the building trades in the AFL, the skilled trades in the auto industry was always a persistent sore spot and irritant to black workers. Long before the civil rights movement in the 1960's manifested the social discontent of black America, black auto workers had expressed their anger and frustration with their treatment and job status. In special UAW conferences on civil rights, at union conventions, at local union meetings and union caucuses, and in forming organizations like the Trade Union Leadership Council, black auto workers articulated their protests over their second-class status. Among the active unionists they were largely accepted, but industry and worker resistance remained formidable.

Much of this unrest was not reflected in written grievances—which are by legal definition a violation of the contract—because the biases against black promotions or transfers or upgrading were a built-in feature of the restrictive seniority systems and other clauses in the contracts. (If a plant had departmentwide seniority in its contract, black workers couldn't break out of the paint shop, or the janitorial department, until the contract was changed, and these changes were violently resisted by affected white workers.)

In the past fifteen years, however, a quantitative change has occurred in black employment in the auto industry. As over one hundred fifty thousand white workers retired under the nego-tiated pension plans, the auto industry boomed in the 1960's, and there were labor market shortages, black employment reached significant proportions by 1972—over two hundred fifty thousand blue-collar workers were black. General Motors had about one hundred thousand or 25 percent of their hourly rated work force; Ford had 35 percent; black employment at Chrysler was about 25 percent.[7]

At this writing in the fall of 1975 at least 25 percent of the black auto workers were still jobless, and in Detroit itself (not the suburbs) unemployment among blacks was conservatively estimated at 30 percent.[8]

The 1967 riot in Detroit in which over 41 persons, mostly black, were killed, 347 injured, and over 3,800 arrested had a greater impact on race relations in the plants after the riot than during the event. It was peaceful in the plants. Nor was there a repetition of 1943 on the streets when thousands of whites roamed around looking for blacks to beat up, with city police concentrating on curbing "niggers." In 1967 looters were both black and white. Less than 10 percent of Detroit's five hundred thousand blacks were involved.[9] Race relations were exacerbated afterward by the hysteria of the white press, the open hostility of the police, always a sore spot now a festering open wound, and a tragic error on the part of Detroit's power structure in trying to revive the city.

The prestigious New Detroit Committee, consisting of top executives of Ford, General Motors, Chrysler, and the business and banking community, decided that the black community leaders were a failure, ignored them, and assisted separatist, nationalist, and supermilitant blacks to become spokesmen for the black community, at least in the media and on the committee. The "new leaders" were well financed, hand-picked by the New Detroit Committee, and in one case imported by the committee from Chicago. The black union leaders who believed in integration were shunted aside, as were the NAACP and the Urban League, from any serious decision making.[10] The consequence was that the more radical and exaggerated the rhetoric, the more attention the black militants received from the committee and the press. The frightened white suburbs were more terrorized, the majority of blacks silenced, and white resistance to integration appeared like a throwback to 1943.

The frictions between blacks and whites took a different form in the auto shops. Where blacks had a majority, they took over the leadership of the plant bargaining units and the local union. My own local union had become 65 percent black by 1972, and three out of four top officers were black. An uneasy truce, or political coalition, existed in plants where the mixture of races was more evenly divided. Eleven local unions in the Detroit area elected black presidents. In the UAW blacks gained staff and executive board positions and a vice president of the union. In Detroit, first a defeat and then a victory brought the first black mayor, Coleman Young, in 1974. He was able to contain a mini-riot in the summer of 1975 from expanding into a major riot.

But the white noose around black Detroit—the divisive race issue in busing, the continued hostility to open housing—keeps race consciousness alive and seething in and out of the plants. The increase from $1 an hour in 1945 to $6.19 an hour in 1975 plus many fringe benefits contained in the UAW-auto industry contracts is by itself a record. But black auto workers, men and women, do have double discontents: the background of race hostility; an inability to live and to send their children to good and peaceful schools; their knowledge that at best white policy is benign neglect, or at worst, who gives a damn. If blue-collar workers resent the stereotype of "Archie Bunker," a brilliant imagination is unnecessary to understand how blacks, auto workers and others, feel about being treated, if not any longer openly as "niggers" certainly still as second-class citizens in many areas on the job, in school, and in home living.

And here, as in so many problems, the limitations of a union as a social force become obvious. The union with perhaps the best record in race relations and policies toward an integrative society finds itself buffeted by cross-political currents, including a strong Wallace sentiment, weakened by mass layoffs and the recession, and functioning in adverse political climate from the standpoint of its program and leadership policies. The UAW leadership supported Coleman Young when he ran for mayor, as they did Richard Austin before that, but few people in Detroit would claim that the UAW leadership spoke for its rank-and-file members on that issue. That's the painful fact that black auto workers live with each day they go into the shop, driving by the homes of auto workers and middle-class whites who don't want them living next door or having their children in the same school, but who must have them, and work with them in the plants, if our industrial complex is to continue functioning.

Notes

1. John G. VanDeusen, *The Black Man in White America* (Washington, D.C.: Associated Publishers, 1944), p. 62.

2. Irving Howe and B. J. Widick, *The UAW and Walter Reuther* (New York: Random House, 1949), p. 209.

3. Ibid., p. 219.

4. B. J. Widick, *Detroit: City of Race and Class Violence* (Chicago: Quadrangle Books, 1972), p. 93.

5. Ibid., p. 126.

6. U.S. Commission on Civil Rights, *Hearing on Housing and Job Discrimination Against Negroes, December 14, 1960* (Detroit, 1960), pp. 87–88.

7. General Motors, Ford, Chrysler Annual Reports to Stockholders, 1973.

8. "Black Unemployment High," *Detroit Free Press,* May 7, 1975.

9. Widick, *Detroit,* p. 167.

10. "Ditto Adapts his Militancy to Golf Course," *Detroit Free Press,* August 26, 1973.

6

Job Satisfaction: A Critique *

Al Nash

Beginning with the Industrial Revolution and persisting to the present day, the quality of working life (QWL) has drawn the attention of academicians, reformers and revolutionaries. With the spread of industrialization, interest has increased, and in recent years there has been a flood of studies of the QWL and the conditions that influence it. In 1972 the three-week strike of the General Motors workers over speedup in a new plant in Lordstown, Ohio, sparked nationwide curiosity and concern with conditions of working life in auto plants and in the workplace generally. It was also a reminder that the auto worker, despite high pay and other benefits, remains among the most militant and angry members of the American labor movement.

The condition of workers on the automobile assembly line has inspired artists, writers, and others to express their protest, and one thinks of the hapless hero of Chaplin's film *Modern Times*, the robots of Capek's play *RUR*, and the phantasmic assembly lines in Huxley's novel *Brave New World*. They were undoubtedly influenced by the reports of journalists and others that automobile workers "work like fiends," that they functioned as

* This study has been abbreviated to accommodate the size of this book. The full-length study is expected to be published.

if they were "robots," that they worked "sixty to seventy hours a week under an unbearable speed-up," that they were "half-dead with fatigue" at the end of the day, and that as a result they were "gutted at forty." Walker and Guest as late as 1952 designated the auto assembly line as "The classic symbol of the subjection of man to the machine in our industrial age."[1] Reports of this nature and the response of scholars and artists (not to mention socialists and union organizers) helped to place the QWL on the social agenda.

The workers who were considered "robots," "half-dead," and "gutted at forty" nevertheless managed to unionize the industry and open up the possiblity of improving the QWL. Their union, the UAW, with a well-deserved reputation for responding to the needs of its members, has represented them for nearly forty years and has had an impact on the QWL in auto plants. Within the industry during these years there have been changes in technology, size of plants, economic practices, and ideology of owners, managers, and supervisors, all of which probably have had implications for the QWL in auto plants. Because of the union, the changes in the industry, and cultural changes in the broader society, four interrelated questions may be asked: What is the QWL of workers on auto, tractor, truck, and engine assembly lines? (Because the technological process and social consequences appear to be similar, we will hereafter refer to "auto assembly lines" for lines assembling autos, tractors, trucks, and engines.) To what extent has it improved since the 1930's? What explanation for the QWL may be found? What are some of the proposals for improving the QWL in auto plants?

Design

There is little agreement on the definition of the QWL, although expressions such as self-fulfillment, self-growth, self-actualization, dignity, interesting work, and job involvement are often used. Most writers subsume these terms under the discussion of job satisfaction and use them to elaborate on what they mean by or what leads to satisfaction. These terms are used by Blauner, whose conceptual framework may be used—with some modification—to systematically assess the QWL. He uses the concept of alienation as a tool for analyzing the QWL in various work settings. Blauner employs a "multidimensional" definition of alienation in order to test its presence among workers. He suggests that alienation develops when a worker experiences powerlessness, meaninglessness, isolation, and self-estrangement.[2] Blauner includes or implies in his conceptual framework the nonalienated pole or the state of freedom that exists when a worker feels he controls his job to a large extent, finds purpose and meaning in his work, is integrated in his work group or organization, and can, as a result, experience growth and feel fulfilled on the job. For our purposes, we will use his multidimensional definition of alienation and the implied definition of freedom as indicators for identifying the QWL. We propose that the QWL is high when the worker feels in fair control of himself, his work, and the social and physical elements in the work site and that the QWL is low when the worker feels he has little or no control of himself, his work, and the social and physical elements in the work site.

Blauner stresses technology, division of labor, economic structure, and social organization, which as independent variables determine to a large extent social behavior in industrial organizations. (Blauner leaves some room for the influence of individual personalities "and character of the labor force in particular industries.") These vary from industry to industry, and an understanding of them and their impact may account for the uneven distribution of the feelings of alienation and freedom found in industry. While Blauner makes some very brief references to the relationship of unions to alienation and freedom in the industrial setting, his conceptual framework makes no provision for this relationship, nor does it provide a function for working conditions in industry and how they may affect alienation and freedom.[3] Therefore, I have added the last two intervening variables to make this approach more relevant for my purposes.

Table 2 summarizes thirteen major articles or books that deal with aspects of the QWL in auto assembly-line plants. It reveals

63

Table 2. Thirteen Major Studies or Articles About Assembly-Line Auto Workers

Author	Year	Method	Population (site, Number)	Worker Satisfaction Yes	No
Howe & Widick	1949	Part.–Obser. social critic	Detroit. Widick worked at Chrysler		X
Walker & Guest	1952	Quant. ran. samp. interviews	Mass. G.M. 180 workers; cross-section		X
Chinoy	1955	Part.-Obser. interviews sociologist	Olds., Lansing, 62 workers; cross-section		X
Marquart	1959	Part.-Obser. social critic	Detroit, generally worked at Briggs		X
Swados	1963	Part.-Obser. social critic	Mahwah, N.J., worked at Ford		X
Blauner	1964	Secondary sources sociologist	Based mainly on Roper rpts. of 180 auto wrks.		X(?)
Kornhauser	1965	Quant. ran. samp. interviews social psych.	Detroit (13 plants) 655 workers cross-section	X(?)	
Shepard	1969	Quant. ran. samp. interviews sociologist	120 auto ass. wrks. & 117 maint. craftsmen; 92 monitors (oil refinery)		X
Form	1973	Quant. ran. samp. sociologist	GM, Olds., Lansing cross-section	X	
Serrin	1973	Some interviews	Detroit		X
Guest	1973	Quant. ran. samp. Interviews	Framingham, Mass. 180 GM workers		X
Siassi et al.	1973	Quant. ran. samp. interviews	GM, Balto., 1,026 wrks., inc. spouses; cross-section	X	
Rothschild	1974	Secondary sources journalist	GM, Lordstown[7]		X

that the methods used by the writers to obtain their data can be divided into three categories. Four studies used participant-observer methods, with the author spending as little as three weeks to as much as fifteen years in a plant. Three of these participants are social critics (Widick, Marquart, Swados), and a fourth is a sociologist (Chinoy) who applies standard sociological concepts to gain perspective and insight. Howe, who collaborated with Widick, the participant-observer of the team, was then and is now a literary and a social critic. A second category consists of two recent studies written by journalists: Rothschild and Serrin. Their accounts are based on secondary sources and some scattered interviews. Their contributions may be described as good and imaginative reporting. A third category in which seven of the studies fall, Walker and Guest, Form, Kornhauser, Shepard, Blauner, Guest, and Siassi, et al., are based on quantitative analysis.

Self-Estrangement

Of the thirteen articles and books, ten indicate that workers are dissatisfied (one of the ten is ambivalent) and three that they are satisfied with their QWL (one of the three is ambivalent). The distribution of opinion reflects the fact that jobs frequently have agreeable as well as disagreeable attributes, so that work is neither an ode to joy nor completely alienating. How the range of attributes of many jobs is perceived depends on the worker's level of expectations, the fit between the worker and the job, his need for a job (or his ability to get another one), how he is making out relative to other workers, and his background. Sometimes the researcher's tendency to substitute his values for the worker's values (ethnomorphising) or his failure to probe deeply may determine what aspects of the job he considers positive or negative. So, not surprisingly, several points of view are found among investigators. Some even have reservations about whether their findings demonstrate that workers are satisfied or dissatisfied with their jobs.

Many writers in describing life on the assembly line use such phrases as "the most hated place in the auto factory"; "The assembly-line is the classic symbol of the subjection of man to the machine"; "Without dissent, assembly-line work was looked upon as the most exacting and most strenuous"; "Almost without exception, the men with whom I worked on the assembly-line felt like trapped animals"; [The workers had] the highest level of dissatisfaction in all industry"; "[The auto worker was characterized by] depersonalization, robotization and a sense of alienation from the total productive process"; and "The auto industry is the *locus classicus* of dissatisfying work; the assembly-line, its quintessential embodiment."[4] These findings indicate a fairly high consistency of opinion and also reveal how shocked the writers are with the work process they find the workers subjected to.

Guest, who in 1973 replicated the classic study he and Walker did of the GM plant in Framingham, Massachusetts, in 1952, notes that most of the 180 auto assemblers he interviewed were hostile to the company. As one of the workers he interviewed protests, "You're just a badge number pushing the line." The comments of these workers were not basically different, says Guest, from those of the workers he and Walker interviewed in 1952. He concludes: "Alienation is not a myth."[5]

Shepard, who compares 120 auto assemblers with 117 maintenance craftsmen in the same auto plant and 92 monitors in an oil refinery, reports that only 14 percent of the assembly-line workers were highly satisfied with their work as compared to 52 percent of the monitors and 87 percent of the maintenance craftsmen. He concludes that functional specialization, as represented by assembly-line jobs, and job satisfaction are negatively related.[6]

Given these characterizations, it is not surprising that the word "dignity," a term often used by unions in their appeal to unorganized and organized workers alike, frequently appears in the literature.[7] The *New York Times* reports that during the worker-student revolt in France in 1968, "striking workers put up signs outside their factories bearing one word, 'dignity.'" In Italy, there was similar behavior during the "hot summer" of 1969.[8] As one of the delegates to a UAW convention said, "Pension plans are fine. That helps the people who retire. SUB plans are fine. It helps the people who are laid off. But we who go into the plant walls have a long way to go in attaining the full citizenship or the dignity of workers that we are entitled to."[9]

The auto worker's search for dignity makes him a "griper," who is not afraid to talk back to the foreman, who doesn't hesitate to submit grievances through his steward or to resort to wildcat strikes and other "illegitimate" means of controlling the work process. Guest says the auto worker's dissatisfaction with his dignity on the job is expressed in the high level of quits, formal grievances, absenteeism, and other indicators. Still another reason for the low state of dignity in auto plants may be the belief prevalent among workers that jobs on the line do not require "brain work"; or as the common saying in auto plants goes, "You need a strong back and weak mind to work here." In part, the workers reflect the opinion of the men who created the assembly line. Henry Ford is quoted as saying, "The assembly line is a haven for those who haven't got the brains to do anything else."[10]

Whatever decade the study is written in, the author finds young workers most dissatisfied. Walker and Guest made that point. Swados comments on a profit-sharing plan introduced by the UAW at American Motors in Milwaukee that mostly younger workers complain "about being made to work too hard, profit-sharing or not profit-sharing." Kornhauser, who analyzed the work and adjustment on assembly and nonassembly-line jobs, reports that only 36 percent of the younger workers on the assembly line were positive in their attitudes toward their jobs as compared to 78 percent of younger workers on nonassembly-line jobs. Guest notes that younger workers quit more often, absent themselves more frequently, and file more official grievances. Drawing a portrait of International Harvester UAW Local 6 in Chicago, an old and militant local, Rosenberg finds that young workers are much more dissatisfied than those of a decade ago.[11]

Blauner, who compared auto workers to three other occupations, finds the auto assembly-line worker highly alienated, but hedges his conclusions. He argues that the auto worker may be self-estranged, but will not exhibit dissatisfaction with his job unless he has a need for "control, initiative and meaning in work," traits which, he says, tend to be associated with the more educated. In presenting this reservation, he touches on a subject of continuing debate among those who believe that workers are dissatisfied and those who believe that they are basically satisfied despite or because of their jobs—with their new freezers, their homes, their vacation trips, and the access they have to the good life.[12] Whatever Blauner's reservations about the relationship of self-estrangement to job satisfaction, he is quite clear about the role of powerlessness in the work situation.

Powerlessness

Blauner points to the powerlessness of the worker, that is, his inability to control his workpace, his physical movement, the use of tools or techniques, and the quality and quantity of work as the most important single factor inducing job dissatisfaction. Blauner emphasizes—as do most writers—that the assembly line essentially determines this powerlessness. As the Shelley report, an economic study of auto and other industries, indicates, the line makes it possible to program the auto assembler down to the last second and for a full 480 minutes of work each day. Chinoy, who explored how automobile workers adjust to the frustrating limitations of their work by redefining the American dream of equal opportunity, says that the worker in an auto plant surrenders control over his behavior for that period of time for which he is compensated. Shepard finds a strong relationship between functional specialization represented by the line and "perceived powerlessness on the job," noting that 93 percent of his sample of auto assemblers expressed a sense of powerlessness as compared to 19 percent of craftsmen in auto and 57 percent of oil refinery monitors.[13]

Speedup, a major cause of powerlessness and the great fear of assembly-line workers, as I found it, is not a process that management carries on uniformly and throughout the line. It may be introduced piecemeal, involving a sprinkling of workers here and there on the line. It may occur on "blue Monday" or payday when many workers are absent. For example, the pace of the line itself may be slowed down as more operations are given to each worker than he feels he can handle. The speedup is often, then, the result of management forcing the workers to carry more operations and to exert more physical effort in the same period of time. It is simply the "buck" on the line moving inexorably toward the worker demanding its tithe of work, which leads him to say, "It's man against machine and it's hard to lick it." [14]

Many writers emphasize the unceasing pace of repetitive qualities of the line, but fail to note the rapidity of the line, which forces workers to labor at top speed. One mishap or one poor tool places a worker "in the hole," that is, behind in his work. [15] This causes other workers on the line to move away from their assigned stations, and they, in turn, fall "in the hole." Each worker is forced to invade the next worker's allotted space, and a good part of the line falls into confusion.

Another type of speedup is associated with the sequence of styles and types of car bodies or motors as they parade down the line. A change in the order of the sequence may bunch up a particular type of motors and force much harder work in the time that was originally allotted by the time and motion engineer, even though the speed of the line remains the same. [16]

Given the incessant and demanding pressures, it is not surprising that an assembly-line worker at the end of the day's work may say, "You follow that iron horse all day and your ass is dragging when you walk out." Or as a Lordstown worker comments, "A good day's work is being tired but not exhausted." [17]

"Fighting the line" sharply increases when new models are introduced. [18] Since there are new parts, new procedures, and new tools the company introduces new work standards for the new model year, which in turn create considerable controversy between the workers and their stewards on one side and the supervisors on the other. At this period the chance of walkouts over charges of speedup are greater.

Marquart, a former local union education director and Briggs worker, writing in 1961 when some Detroit Chrysler workers for the first time demanded the ouster of the UAW from their plant, said that despite the changes in technology and the introduction of automation, older union members informed him that "speedup is now more intense than at any time since the thirties." Rothschild, whose book is devoted to demonstrating that the automobile industry is in decline, also refers to automation and points out that despite the construction of a new plant at Lordstown and the installation by GM of the latest technological devices, workers still work as hard as ever and do menial tasks while the machines perform the skilled and semiskilled jobs. "Fordism," she says, still lives in Lordstown producing in addition to cars, monotony, fragmentation of work, speedup, sabotage, and absenteeism. Swados, a novelist and former worker at the Ford plant in Mahwah, New Jersey, in reporting his reservations about the effectiveness of the UAW in combating the line, questions the belief that the introduction of automation has led or will lead to raising the "workers' level of skill, responsibility and initiative." Faunce, who studied automation in the auto industry and who Swados quotes as an authority, says that "automation has not altered the fact that most production-line jobs do not produce the kind of occupational involvement or identification necessary to make work a satisfying experience." [19]

Commenting also on automation, Serrin, who writes about the "civilized relationship" between GM and the UAW, an ironical characterization, notes that it has "eased some of the work," but adds that to many workers, "automation is an enemy" because it has increased production and added more duties to their jobs. [20] Apparently, automating assembly lines, whether in 1961, 1963, or 1973, has had little positive impact on the QWL.

Other problems that workers feel relatively powerless to deal with are compulsory overtime, transfers to other jobs on the line, the right to be absent without a doctor's excuse, and shift preference. For example, in more prosperous days, assembly-line workers frequently went on strike or walked out over the right to reject compulsory overtime without being punished. As Rothschild notes, in a plant such as Lordstown, a worker "must ask and wait for permission to get married on Saturday," or bring a note from the funeral director saying that he attended his father's funeral. Rothschild claims that this kind of arbitrary relationship leads, as one of the Lordstown workers said to her, to "one, American law outside the plant, and a GM law inside," and, as a result, contributes to the "dehumanization" of the worker.[21]

Another aspect of powerlessness, the large size of auto factories, is noted by a number of writers. Almost 55 percent of auto workers are employed in factories with more than twenty-five hundred workers.[22] These plants are larger than plants in printing, textiles, chemicals, shipbuilding, and other industries. Their size fosters a feeling of powerlessness among auto workers. Workers feel there are no lines of communication between them and the invisible company executives; they feel helpless confronting a company that acts like the fabled many-headed Hydra. Thus, a strike in one company plant may result in the shift of work to another company plant. Win one speedup grievance by a walkout and soon the company will confront another group of workers with another speedup.[23]

Bigness and power are, of course, related to bureaucratic structure and management ability to utilize this structure to control the working lives of its employees. In labor-management relations, this control is legitimated in management prerogatives that are formalized in collective bargaining agreements and give management the "inalienable right," for example, to set production standards, to transfer work to other plants, to schedule overtime, to regulate the speed of the line, to close a plant—even if subject to some modifications by the collective bargaining agreement.[24]

Meaninglessness

A typical assembly-line worker can learn his job in thirty minutes. He gains no skill that might qualify him for a better job. He has little incentive, investigators claim, to acquire the "instincts of workmanship," to take pride in his job, or to feel a sense of purpose. Not only is the worker confronted with a sense of meaninglessness; he cannot engage in reveries because the work requires close attention and resists the kind of detachment that permits the mind to wander. Blauner states that the auto assembler is more alienated than any other worker by the feeling of meaninglessness associated with his work. He has neither a sense of purpose nor an identification with the company, and he feels himself an insignificant part of the process of production.[25] In sum, the character of the product, the extremely limited scope of the tasks, and the bureaucratic organization of work creates a Procrustean bed in which the worker—like the victims of Procrustes—is apparently tailored to fit the needs of his master, the line.

Isolation

The anonymity and remoteness of management, the size of the plant, the intricate bureaucratic structure, the standardization of tasks, and the fragmentation of work give the worker little loyalty to or integration in the company.[26]

In addition, the inability of workers to climb up the company ladder[27] emphasizes their feelings of depersonalization, anonymity, and atomization.[28] There is little progression in wages among auto assembly-line workers. As Shelley points out, at the most there is a two-step progression and in general the relative dispersion of wages in auto is the lowest of all industry. The weak normative integration of worker and management is further aggravated by the fact that few workers are able to become foremen, according to Fullan, who compared worker integration in Canadian auto, printing, and oil plants. Also, few auto workers have hopes of or interest in becoming foremen.[29]

Even automation and/or increased mechanization of the line do not increase the possibilities of promotion; in fact, Marquart finds that such opportunities are narrowed. Thus, it is argued that neither the pattern of relations between foremen and workers nor the possibilities of promotion contribute significantly to the normative integration of workers in the company. These conditions help to enlarge the cleavage between workers and management and the conflict that follows.[30]

Another aspect of isolation is reflected in the infrequent interaction between workers and supervisor. Nearly half the sample of 180 workers interviewed by Walker and Guest reported they had contact with their respective foremen "less than once a month." One reason for this infrequent interaction is suggested by Fullan, who notes that the foreman is responsible for a fairly large number of workers, certainly as compared to foremen in the printing and oil industries. He suggests that this contributes to the poor integration of the auto workers in the company. [31]

Still another factor that increases isolation is the absence of a warm and rewarding relationship within the occupation or group. This is due, in part, it is claimed, to the difficulty of developing a cohesive and stable group on assembly-line operations. The arrangement of isolated tasks and the awesome noises, writers point out, do not permit much interaction on the line, either of a technical or social nature. Form, for example, finds that assembly-line workers tend to have the least interaction of all auto workers. He also indicates that as compared to skilled auto workers, auto assemblers find work more satisfying when they have frequent opportunity to talk to one another on the job. Fullan notes that members of other occupations interact with one another more frequently than do auto assemblers. Faunce interviewed 125 workers employed on an automated assembly line who had previously worked on the assembly line for the same company in another plant and reports that the workers on the automated line had less interaction among themselves as well as with their foreman than on their prior jobs. [32] In general, then, these writers find that weak normative integration of workers in the company stimulates intensive labor-management conflict.

Self-Fulfillment

Siassi and his associates compared the mental health of UAW workers employed at various skills in the Baltimore plant of GM. They divided their respondents into those who received psychiatric assistance and those who did not and found little significant difference between the two groups. A substantial majority in both groups reported that they were satisfied with their jobs. Summarizing their findings, Siassi et al. state that there was little loneliness or life dissatisfaction among their respondents and consider their findings a tribute to the workers' ability satisfactorily to survive the factory milieu and not to the jobs provided by the assembly line. [33]

Form, who made a comparative study of auto workers in the United States, Italy, India, and Argentina, is another writer who finds auto assemblers and other occupational groups in the auto plant satisfied with their work. He notes that skilled workers are much more highly satisfied than unskilled assembly-line workers, but also reports the assembly-line workers as "satisfied." [34] Form suggests that assembly-line workers along with other unskilled workers are satisfied with the money they make, with the location of their work, with their contact with other workers, and with their work routines. He believes that "most workers have come to terms with their jobs." Form is critical of the findings of Chinoy, Blauner, Walker and Guest, and others who claim that workers are alienated and suggests that it is necessary to reconsider the belief that routinized, mechanical work leads to self-estrangement. [35]

In a slightly different category are writers who acknowledge that auto workers are satisfied with the QWL but, like Kornhauser, argue that dissatisfied workers rarely will openly admit to dissatisfaction. Kornhauser, who concedes that his findings indicate auto assemblers are satisfied with their work and life experience, finds that the positive responses must be treated cautiously for they are moderate, passive, and unenthusiastic. Few auto workers, Kornhauser indicates, like their jobs as compared to other jobs they know or would pick if they "could go back to the age of 15 and start all over again." [36]

The problem of characterizing the degree of satisfaction or self-fulfillment workers have with their jobs is, as Kornhauser implies, not neatly disposed of. Thus Blauner, who reports that a cross-section of two thousand auto workers indicated that their jobs were interesting "most or all of the time," nevertheless questions the significance of the findings and argues that the satisfaction of a worker with a job may be the result of stagnating on the job or accepting "the lack of challenge in his work environment." Workers are satisfied, but perhaps they should be dissatisfied, he appears to suggest. [37]

Blauner is ambivalent. While he admits that the auto worker experiences more powerlessness, isolation, meaninglessness, and self-estrangement on the job than people in other occupations, in the end, he says, high pay and job security reduce discontent with work processes and result "in moderate satisfaction with the job as a whole" even if the auto worker feels "strong dissatisfaction with the actual work routines." In the final analysis, the auto assembler, the near "classic model of the self-estranged worker," adapts to the line. In reaching this conclusion, he joins Chinoy in claiming that the auto worker is "in a sense, trapped by the high pay and the lack of alternatives." [38]

Bell, who discusses alienation and bureaucracy, is not too far from Blauner's position in criticizing sociologists who collect survey data to prove that workers are satisfied with their work, when in fact they may be satisfied not with their work but with other aspects of their situation such as the group with which they work. His major point, however, is that unless the sociologists give the worker an alternative to compare with his present job, the questions about job satisfaction represent neither "meaningful" nor "real" choices. [39]

Berger, on the other hand, who carried out a study of one hundred Ford auto workers dwelling in a semirural area near San Jose, California, is critical of those whom he accuses of substituting their own values for those of the workers. In effect, he accuses Chinoy and left-wing critics of saying to workers, "Your standards are inferior, your happiness is illusory, your material comforts meaningless and your family life is impoverished." [40]

The preceding statement and findings suggest that the comments on self-fulfillment are meager. If self-fulfillment takes place, it is not on the job, the studies claim, but rather the access which the job permits to achieving satisfaction outside the plant. Of sixty-two workers Chinoy interviewed, forty-eight expressed a desire to leave the plant. Their idea of self-fulfillment was, for example, to buy a home, a car, and other consumer goods, to go into business, to enter college, or to be an independent farmer; self-fulfillment is located somewhere in the world outside the workplace. In the meantime, Chinoy reports, the opportunity to earn relatively high wages enables the worker to endure disagreeable and arduous work. The money enables him to acquire the personal possessions which he identifies with getting ahead.[41]

Form also stresses the importance of money for assembly-line workers by suggesting that they would rather have "more money than sociability" and that their reason for liking the job is "money." Walker and Guest also emphasize wages and fringe benefits as a major reason for liking the job and working in the plant, while Guest, twenty-one years after his joint study with Walker, reports that wages and fringe benefits are more important than ever to keep the workers in the plant.[42]

Control (Power)

Only Form finds that the assemblers do not object to their inability to control the job. He reports more workers complain about working conditions than about pace of work, lack of responsibility, or lack of control.[43]

Meaningfulness

As with the category of control, few writers present examples of assembly-line workers who find intrinsic meaning in their work. Chinoy quotes an assembler as saying, "I have an appreciation of myself when I do a good job," and suggests that he and others may derive satisfaction from doing "an honest day's work." In addition, the challenge of facing the line often gives the worker a feeling of accomplishment, as if he had performed a feat.[44] Aside from these comments, little else is said of meaningfulness.

Integration

The line provides a superb form of technical and impersonal control for management. One of the latent functions of the line is that it makes it unnecessary for the foreman to act primarily as a "pusher." As one auto worker says: "The average guy fighting the line has two foremen. One is the regular foreman, the other is the damn line itself. They both keep pushing you." It creates an additional role for the foreman in which, to some extent, he acts as a trouble-shooter or a problem-solver engaging less in giving orders. Consequently, conditions emerge that permit the foreman to maintain a more friendly relationship between himself and the worker.[45]

Goldthorpe, who claims there has been too much emphasis on technology as a determinant in analyzing workers' behavior in the plant and therefore suggests that consideration be given to attitudes held by workers before entering the plant in order to understand their definition of their work situation, reports that, despite onerous conditions on the assembly line, there is little antagonism between worker and foreman. In distinguishing his findings from other studies that also report little antagonism between workers and foreman, Goldthorpe points out that his assemblers have only "infrequent contact" with the foreman. He argues that individuals who look at their work instrumentally, as do auto assemblers, prefer an impersonal and remote relationship with foremen and have less need for praise and approval from them.[46]

Form, commenting on the relationship between technology and the social behavior of auto workers in four countries, reports that the quantity and quality of social interaction was high for most workers (including assemblers) and that most were satisfied with the kind of contact they had with others on the job. Yet, he argues, "it is possible for workers to be highly integrated at work and feel powerless about events in society." He concludes that there is no direct relationship between the feeling of anomie and social relations in the work setting and suggests that there is now sufficient evidence to lead us to "modify or abandon technological explanations of alienation or anomie."[47]

Working Conditions

Working conditions form the major component of the environment in which the worker spends most of his waking day and significantly contribute to the degree of satisfaction or dissatisfaction the worker has with his QWL. Perhaps the only favorable comment on safety, health standards, and other working conditions of auto assemblers is that of Walker and

Guest, who conclude that as a whole the workers in their sample were satisfied with conditions such as lighting, level of noise, ventilation, safety, cleanliness, temperature, and the services of the cafeteria, although they acknowledge that those satisfactory conditions did not compensate the workers for the unattractiveness of the job. The plant they studied was only two years old and its newness may account for the positive attitude of the workers. On the other hand, Kornhauser reports that 60 percent of his respondents made unfavorable comments about such working conditions as dirt, noise, heat, and safety. Sexton and Sexton also illustrate the quality of working conditions by quoting a student who obtained a summer job in an auto plant. He describes his place of work as a "bewildering maze of complicated machinery, conveyor belts, smoke and steam," adding that "the cacophony of roaring, whirring, pounding, whistling noises is painful to your ears." In a similar vein, Serrin characterized Detroit auto plants as "hot clangorous places, often filled with smoke and stenches." 48

Wallick, a UAW staff member, refers to a report made by Edith Van Horn, also a UAW staff member and a former shop steward at Dodge (Detroit) who says that "at least 80 percent of my grievances were directly related to the health and safety of my women—like the fight for gloves, for protective clothing, doors on the toilets, protection from fumes." In addition, she lists complaints against excessive drafts, standing on concrete floors, insufficient water fountains, poor food on lunch wagons, poor facilities for hanging clothes, and lack of toilet paper, soap, and other important items. 49

To this list of working problems are added observations I made as a worker and as a chief steward of the motor line at the Chrysler East Jefferson Plant in Detroit (1949-53). The roofs frequently leaked when it rained, soaking the workers on the assembly line below; overhead pipes sweated in the winter and rained down on the workers. In the summer the sun shone through the skylights causing vision problems. During lunchtime or on a break there was always difficulty finding a place to sit or to rest. In other departments, I remember that the air was frequently saturated with dust, a derivative of spraying or of metal buffing, which provoked more walkouts than the speed of the line.

Bluestone, a UAW vice president and director of its GM department, suggests that workers feel relatively deprived when they compare their working conditions with those of management. Bluestone, whose article is devoted to the participation of workers in decision making on the job, calls the preferred treatment management receives the "double standard" and lists the "symbols of elitism" as salaries (rather than hourly rates), paneled dining rooms, the absence of a time clock, and the provision of special and convenient parking areas for their cars. 50

Workers on the afternoon and the night shifts also feel deprived and share the same discomforts of the day shift, but have less resources for coping with them. (I make this assertion on the basis of the years of experience in observing the work life of the day shift and that of the afternoon shift.) In addition, many of them are trapped on their shifts and feel isolated from their families and friends. They often feel a loss of self-esteem, considerable anxiety, and conflicting pressures as a result of being deprived of a normal social and family life. In general, then, afternoon and night-shift workers may feel more powerless and more discontented with their conditions of work than day-shift workers.

Critical Evaluation

With the exception of a few, writers fail to examine closely the warp and woof of the QWL in assembly-line departments and especially those aspects in work that soften the impact of the assembly line and prevent the "dehumanization" of workers. To examine the implications of this statement, I begin with my own experience as a chief steward and worker on the motor line in Chrysler. I can only recall two walkouts in five years in the motor line department. Neither of the walkouts grew out of the pressure of the line. One walkout related to the refusal of a new worker to join the union, the other was over the failure of the company to patch up the roof so that rain would not pour down on the workers below. While workers always exhibited distrust about the speed of the line, many grievances filed by those I represented (approximately eight hundred workers in my department) were about management's effort to discipline them for lateness, absences, drinking, insubordination, or other matters not directly related to the character of the assembly line. Complaints, for example, were often made about the absence of wooden slats to walk on, "short days," compulsory overtime, the length of time it took to answer a grievance, absence of protective gloves, arbitrary transfers, and the need for fans and salt tablets in the summer. Complaints about the line occurred on Mondays or Fridays (payday) when large numbers of workers were absent and the speed of the line was *reduced*, a change accompanied by increasing the workload of each worker. But in general the problems relating to the line and the charges of dehumanization do not appear to have loomed large in terms of specific grievances—although the line set the ambience for the workers in the department and in the plant.

Dehumanization

Dehumanization is associated with the loss of one's identity, the feeling of demoralization, debasement, degradation, humiliation, and mortification, or of robotlike conduct. It is a process frequently found in total institutions such as prisons, mental hospitals, or mercenary nursing homes for the aged and is produced by tyrannization, regimentation, and desocialization. Dehumanization, some claim, exists in auto assembly-line plants. For example, Blauner appears to suggest its existence when he describes the auto assembler as "the worker prototype of the mass man," who in relation to his company and union "is relatively powerless, atomized, depersonalized, and anonymous."[51] Rothschild uses the words "dehumanization of auto industry work" and "degradation of work" to describe the conditions that produced the Lordstown strike of GM workers. [52] Serrin, referring to murals painted in 1933 by Diego Rivera in Detroit depicting work life in auto plants, described the appearance of auto workers in the murals as "grim-faced robots" and "automatons." He adds that almost four decades later, work life in most auto plants "remains in large part as Rivera painted it." Life in the factory "is dull, brutish, weary, stuporous." These comments are typical of how a number of commentators perceive the impact of assembly lines on the auto worker.[53]

I have met auto workers with all kinds of personalities, those who were authoritarians, racists, or company stooges as well as those who were permissive, tolerant, or rebellious. I have never met a worker who resembled the Chaplinesque figure in *Modern Times* or who had characteristics similar to those acquired in prison, nursing homes, or mental institutions or who, as in Blauner's terms, is "atomized, depersonalized, and anonymous." It is quite true that the assembly-line worker is chained in Ixionlike fashion to an assembly line; that the worker is treated with distrust, with cynicism, and in an impersonal fashion, and often reacts in like fashion; that the worker is told that he is stupid, and easily replaceable; that he feels himself often an appendage to the machine and subject to the alien laws of the company. All this is "unnatural," and yet the worker does not become dehumanized.

The very militancy for which the auto assembly-line worker is justly known is a form of control indicating to management that there are limits they dare not trespass lest the workers react in a slowdown or wildcat strike. The militancy of the worker and the common resentment that he shares with his colleagues against the company reduce markedly his degree of estrangement, isolation, meaninglessness, and powerlessness on the job. As limited as the union's control over the assembly has been, the worker nevertheless has been able to use his union constantly for defensive purposes and periodically for offensive purposes.

Mitigating Factors

The workers I knew were hardly cheerful about working on the line and were quick to complain in demanding and in not so gentle tones. They resented the constant demands of the line. But there were also amenities that moderated the harshness of the line and made the QWL tolerable for many workers, especially those with substantial seniority. Some of these amenities were often made possible by senior workers acquiring desirable jobs which gave them a basis for making favorable comparisons.

Some of these amenities grew out of the interstices existing in the technological and bureaucratic structures of the auto corporations. In these areas workers create their own autonomy and control, which they zealously defend, sometimes against the advice of their union stewards. For instance, in the machine shop, the department in which the crankshafts were machined and then conveyed to the motor line on which I worked, most workers would complete their unofficial quotas of work before lunchtime, and a number of them would frequent the men's room where roulette and dice games helped pass the time in a more exciting, if expensive, fashion. They defended their work quotas against the complaints of the company for years and threatened to walk out on several occasions when the company proposed to increase the quota. (The union, while not defending the gambling, fought to protect the quotas which the workers had established.)

In my department, as in others, a small number of men doubled up—an "illegitimate" practice—working a half-hour on and a half-hour off, so that they could play the numbers, sleep, read, or visit their friends. (For recognition of doubling up and related practices for making work more tolerable and satisfactory, see Aronowitz, Blauner, Marquart, Walker and Guest, and Kreman.)[54] Still others worked on jobs off the line, which permitted them to "bank" the work that exceeded the quota for the day. Since "banking" permitted greater control over work than doubling up, the worker on this job by speeding up his pace of work had even more leisure to spend in following his pursuits. In addition many workers did not carry out their tasks in the prescribed manner, but rather developed shortcuts of their own. All of this contributed to making the day pass more rapidly and less monotonously.

Finally, there were also workers who did repairs, performed semiskilled jobs on operations adjacent to the line, or operated easier jobs on the line. They, too, had more control over their efforts and movements than other workers, especially those with little seniority who generally were assigned to the least desirable work.

If assembly-line workers are not quite as powerless as Blauner and others see them, neither are they as atomized as some of the same writers suggest. As my preceding comments intimate, there is far more social interaction on the job or in the department than some investigators report. For instance, as the assembly line snakes its way through the motor department, it forms (in Chrysler, 1953) a bull ring, a "merry-go-round," and separate areas that include balancing, a push line, a repair shop, and couplings. Each section may also have clusters of workers who do exactly the same operation and tend to work as a team, by their own design. In addition, each section is supervised by a foreman. The separation of the line into at least nine segments, each with its own foreman, creates a distinct sense of groupness and with it a consciousness of common interests. Thus, in my capacity as chief steward, I would often meet at lunchtime with members of different segments of the line to discuss their complaints. In general, I only did what other union stewards did in their departments: coordinate groups of workers; process their grievances; persuade them to attend union meetings to defend their interests; and help raise their consciousness of their collective strength.

Of course, groups of workers are formed because of other reasons. Thus, there are ethnic groups, groups of horseplayers, pinochle and gin rummy players, drinkers, personal friends, and those sharing similar political views in the union. I have seen some groups play gin rummy or pinochle every day at lunchtime for over four years. Similar groups are distributed throughout the plant.

Another reason for the existence of identifiable groups is that normally it is difficult to transfer out of the department or to be promoted, as noted above, and consequently workers tend to remain in their original department, perpetuating old ties. 55 Since there are few opportunities to leave, workers accommodate to the social order represented by the department by moving laterally. Once they find a job they like or become accustomed to in the department, they will strongly resist any effort to move them to another job or to add another operation to their job. Part of the accommodation results from having been in the department long enough to have known the foreman when he was a worker and consequently to expect him to be somewhat more considerate of those he knew in more informal circumstances.

Perhaps another illustration of the presence of fairly cohesive groups on the auto assembly line is the well-known phenomenon of walkouts as an expression of intensive conflict in auto assembly-line departments. Walkouts and other expressions of intense conflict could not take place without the presence of cohesiveness and a high degree of worker involvement in the group. Indeed, intense conflict strengthens the structure and cohesion of the group, and in turn, added cohesion and structure make possible the continuation of conflict. [56]

Conflict generated by the workers through the union or their group structure also tends to mitigate the severity of the line, the harshness of working conditions, and the authoritarian impact of management. Conflict reaffirms the humanity of workers; it demonstrates that their will, desires, and interests must be recognized.

Perhaps a major conclusion to draw from this review is that assembly-line workers have learned to some extent to cope with those factors that tend to degrade their work and dehumanize them. If the task of auto assembly-line workers has been a Sisyphean one, they have not been overwhelmed by the persistent pressure of management that ensnares them in technological, economic, and bureaucratic webs. Management continues to hold the throttle of the line in its hands, supported ideologically and legally by the social order, but the workers, by their own efforts and with the help of their union, have demonstrated considerable immunity to the harmful effects of the line.

Thus, Blauner's finding that the auto worker is powerless, isolated, and self-estranged should be modified to recognize the use of the union by workers to protect themselves from the dehumanizing effects of the assembly line and the mitigating factors developed by the workers themselves to reduce the harshness of the line, the unpleasant working conditions, and the insensitive bureaucratic structure.

The QWL in auto assembly plants still is inadequate and far below the expectations of workers. While not as bad as suggested by Blauner and others, and certainly better than in the 1930's, conditions could be much improved. The composition of the workers has changed, too. Some are younger, better educated, more radical or sophisticated, and have higher expectations than their predecessors. [57] What the old-timer of the 1930's saw as a significant improvement is taken for granted by the younger worker. Progress, in the sense of constant improvements of the QWL, has not been continuous; rather, the union and the workers have been forced to retreat in face of the industry's persistent efforts to intensify efficiency and rationalization of work and because of the problems of cost, competition, and unemployment in the industry. Indeed, the union's failure to develop successful tactics to cope with "Fordism" and the prerogatives of management, especially with respect to work standards, has been criticized by many of its old friends. In advocating more vigorous tactics, they never leave doubt that the union is indispensable to the workers' struggles to improve their QWL. But they would also agree with Bell's statement that unions generally have failed to question the present structure of work because "to do so would require a radical challenge to society as a whole."[58]

Notes

1. Robert W. Dunn, *Labor and Automobiles* (New York: International Publishers, 1929), p. 90; Herbert Harris, *American Labor* (New Haven: Yale University Press, 1939), pp. 368, 271; Mary H. Vorse, *Labor's New Millions* (New York: Modern Age Books, 1939), pp. 60, 59; Charles Walker and Robert Guest, *The Man on the Assembly Line* (Cambridge, Mass.: Harvard University Press, 1952), p. 9.

2. Robert Blauner, *Alienation and Freedom: The Factory Worker and His Industry* (Chicago: University of Chicago Press, 1964), pp. 32–44.

3. Ibid., pp. 6–11.

4. Frank Marquart, "The Auto Worker," in *Voices of Dissent* (New York: Grove Press, 1958), p. 144; Walker and Guest, *Man on the Assembly Line*, p. 9; Eli Chinoy, *Automobile Workers and the American Dream* (Boston: Beacon Press, 1955), p. 70; Harvey Swados, "The Myth of the Happy Worker," in E. and M. Josephson, eds., *Man Alone* (New York: Dell, 1962), p. 111; Blauner, *Alienation and Freedom*, p. 121; Irving Howe and B. J. Widick, *The UAW and Walter Reuther* (New York: Random House, 1949), p. 20; U.S. Department of Health, Education, and Welfare, *Work in America: Report of a Special Task Force to the Secretary of Health, Education, and Welfare* (Cambridge, Mass.: MIT Press, 1973), p. 38; John Goldthorpe, "Attitudes and Behavior of Car Assembly Workers: A Deviant Case and a Theoretical Critique," *British Journal of Sociology*, 17 (September 1966), 235.

5. Robert H. Guest, "The Man on the Assembly Line: A Generation Later," *Tuck Today* (May 1973), 4–5.

6. Jon Shepard, "Functional Specialization and Work Attitudes," *Industrial Relations*, 8 (February 1969), 190, 193.

7. Howe and Widick, *The UAW and Walter Reuther;* Walker and Guest, *The Man on the Assembly Line;* Chinoy, *Automobile Workers and the American Dream;* Frank Marquart, "New Problems for the Unions," *Dissent*, 6 (Autumn 1959), 375–88; Harvey Swados, "The UAW—Over the Top or Over the Hill," *Dissent*, 10 (Autumn 1963), 321–43; Blauner, *Alienation and Freedom;* Arthur Kornhauser, *Mental Health of the Industrial Worker* (New York: John Wiley and Sons, 1965); Shepard, "Functional Specialization"; William H. Form, "Auto Workers and Their Machines: A Study of Work, Factory, and Job Satisfaction in Four Countries," *Social Forces*, 52 (September 1973), 1–15; William Serrin, *The Company and the Union* (New York: Alfred A. Knopf, 1973); Guest, "The Man on the Assembly Line," p. 2; Iradj Siassi, Guido Crocetti, and Herzl R. Spiro, "Loneliness and Dissatisfaction in a Blue Collar Population," *Archives of General Psychiatry*, 30 (February 1974), 261–65; Emma Rothschild, *Paradise Lost: The Decline of the Auto-Industrial Age* (New York: Vintage Books, 1974).

8. *New York Times*, June 2, 1975.

9. Marquart, "The Auto Worker," p. 156.

10. Blauner, *Alienation and Freedom*, pp. 121–22; Guest, "Man on the Assembly Line," p. 2; Daniel Bell, *Work and Its Discontents* (Boston: Beacon Press, 1956), p. 249; Irving Bluestone, "Worker Participation in Decision-Making," in Roy F. Fairfield, ed., *Humanizing the Workplace* (Buffalo: Prometheus Books, 1974), p. 53.

11. Walker and Guest, *Man on the Assembly Line*, p. 135; Swados, "Myth of the Happy Worker," p. 324; Kornhauser, *Mental Health*, p. 166; Guest, "Man on the Assembly Line," p. 2; Bernard Rosenberg, "Torn Apart and Driven Together: Portrait of a UAW Local in Chicago," *Dissent*, 19 (Winter 1972), 66.

12. Blauner, *Alienation and Freedom*, p. 122.

13. Ibid., pp. 98–107; E. F. Shelley, and Company, *Climbing the Job Ladder* (New York: E. F. Shelley and Co., 1970), p. 41; Chinoy, *Automobile Workers*, p. 85; Shepard, "Functional Specialization," p. 191.

14. Guest, "Man on the Assembly Line," p. 1.

15. Stanley Aronowitz, *False Promises: The Shaping of the American Working Class* (New York: McGraw-Hill, 1973), p. 23.

16. Blauner, *Alienation and Freedom*, p. 100.

17. Serrin, *Company and the Union*, p. 255; Aronowitz, *False Promises*, 21.

18. Howe and Widick, *UAW and Walter Reuther*, p. 24; Bluestone, "Worker Participation," p. 59.

19. Frank Marquart, "Trouble in Auto," *Dissent,* 8 (Spring 1961), 113; Rothschild, *Paradise Lost,* p. 107; Swados, "The UAW—Over the Top," p. 325; William A. Faunce, "The Automobile Industry: A Case Study in Automation," Chapter 25 in H. B. Jacobson and J. S. Roucek, eds., *Automation and Society* (New York: Philosophical Library, 1959).

20. Serrin, *Company and the Union,* pp. 229–31.

21. Aronowitz, *False Promises,* p. 41; Rothschild, *Paradise Lost,* pp. 115–16.

22. Blauner, *Alienation and Freedom,* p. 92.

23. Marquart, "New Problems for the Unions," pp. 383–85; Swados, "The UAW—Over the Top," p. 326.

24. Marquart, "New Problems for the Unions," p. 383; Swados, "The UAW—Over the Top," pp. 325–26.

25. Rothschild, *Paradise Lost,* p. 131; Blauner, *Alienation and Freedom,* pp. 115, 107.

26. Ibid., pp. 24, 109.

27. Walker and Guest, *Man on the Assembly Line,* Chapter 9.

28. Robert H. Guest, "Work Careers and Aspirations of Automobile Workers," in W. Galenson and S. M. Lipset, eds., *Labor and Trade Unionism* (New York: John Wiley and Sons, 1960), p. 320.

29. Walker and Guest, *Man on the Assembly Line,* pp. 160–61; Chinoy, *Automobile Workers,* p. 38; Blauner, *Alienation and Freedom,* p. 111; Shelley, *Climbing the Job Ladder,* pp. 47–49; Michael Fullan, "Industrial Technology and Worker Integration in the Organization," *American Sociological Review,* 35 (December 1970), 1031.

30. Marquart, "New Problems for the Unions," p. 382.

31. Walker and Guest, *Man on the Assembly Line,* p. 93; Fullan, "Industrial Technology," p. 1033.

32. Blauner, *Alienation and Freedom,* p. 109; Form, "Auto Workers and Their Machines," p. 13; Fullan, "Industrial Technology," p. 1032; William A. Faunce, "Automation in the Automobile Industry: Some Consequences for the Plant Social Structure," *American Sociological Review,* 23 (August 1958), 404.

33. Siassi, et al., "Loneliness and Dissatisfaction," p. 262.

34. Form, "Auto Workers and Their Machines," pp. 1–15.

35. Ibid., pp. 5, 13–14.

36. Kornhauser, *Mental Health,* pp. 9–10, 57–61, 158.

37. Blauner, *Alienation and Freedom,* pp. 117–118, 204.

38. Ibid., pp. 119–22.

39. Daniel Bell, "Work, Alienation, and Social Control," *Dissent,* 21 (Spring 1974), 210n.

40. Bennett Berger, *Working-Class Suburb* (Berkeley: University of California Press, 1960), p. 103.

41. Chinoy, *Automobile Workers,* p. 133; Eli Chinoy, "Manning the Machines—The Assembly Line Worker," in Peter L. Berger, ed., *The Human Shape of Work* (New York: Macmillan Co., 1964), p. 75.

42. Form, "Auto Workers and Their Machines," pp. 1–15; Walker and Guest, *Man on the Assembly Line,* Chapter 6; Guest, "Man on the Assembly Line," p. 4.

43. Form, "Auto Workers and Their Machines," pp. 11–12.

44. Chinoy, *Automobile Workers,* p. 131; Aronowitz, *False Promises,* p. 23.

45. Guest, "Man on the Assembly Line," p. 4; Walker and Guest, *Man on the Assembly Line,* p. 99; Blauner, *Alienation and Freedom,* p. 107.

46. Goldthorpe, "Attitudes and Behavior," p. 234.

47. William H. Form, "Technology and Social Behavior in Four Countries: A Sociotechnical Perspective," *American Sociological Review*, 37 (December 1972), 737.

48. Walker and Guest, *Man on the Assembly Line*, pp. 102–5; Kornhauser, *Mental Health*, pp. 172–73; Patricia Cayo Sexton and Brendon Sexton, *Blue Collar and Hard Hats* (New York: Random House, 1971), p. 164; Serrin, *Company and the Union*, pp. 223–34.

49. Frank Wallick, *The American Worker: An Endangered Species* (New York: Ballantine Books, 1972), p. 164.

50. Bluestone, "Worker Participation," p. 58.

51. Blauner, *Alienation and Freedom*, p. 122.

52. Rothschild, *Paradise Lost*, pp. 116, 166.

53. Serrin, *Company and the Union*, p. 221.

54. Aronowitz, *False Promises*, pp. 23–24; Blauner, *Alienation and Freedom*, pp. 99–100; Marquart, "The Auto Worker," p. 144; Walker and Guest, *Man on the Assembly Line*, pp. 146–47; Bennett Kreman, "Search for a Better Way of Work: Lordstown, Ohio," in Fairfield, ed., *Humanizing the Workplace*, pp. 146–47.

55. Chinoy, *Automobile Workers*, p. 124.

56. Lewis A. Coser, *The Function of Social Conflict* (Glencoe, Ill.: Free Press, 1956), Chapter 5.

57. Wallick, *The American Worker*, p. 76; Aronowitz, *False Promises*, pp. 26–27; Andrew Levison, *The Working Class Majority* (New York: Coward, McCann, and Geoghegan, 1974), p. 215; Kreman, "Search for a Better Way of Work," p. 149.

58. Bell, "Work, Alienation, and Social Control," p. 211.

7

Summary and Conclusions

by B. J. Widick

In reflecting on the realities of workers' attitudes and social relations in the auto factories and in reviewing the variety and complexity of problems and the sources of friction and anxieties that exist there, the participants in this study concluded that neither a hypothesis based on the concepts of "job satisfaction" nor "alienation" alone offered a satisfactory basis for analysis and judgment. Neither approaches factors in the totality of and the wide differences in the causes of job discontents, nor the many variables that affect workers in the auto industry. The feelings of most workers about their jobs tend to form a continuum between job satisfaction and alienation rather than polarization around either concept.

As Nash has pointed out in his working paper, "There is little agreement on the definition of the QWL, although expressions such as self-fulfillment, self-growth, self-actualization, dignity, interesting work, and job involvement are often used. Most writers subsume these terms under the discussion of job satisfaction and use them to elaborate on what they mean by satisfaction or what leads to satisfaction." Nash's review of thirteen major studies or articles about assembly-line auto workers indicates the limitations inherent in that approach.

Nash's comments, in his section on self-estrangement, indicate that ten of the thirteen studies found worker dissatisfaction. He concluded that other factors than the actual job affected workers' feelings and that the investigators' findings may have been colored by their own views. Thus the findings are not conclusive demonstrations of worker satisfaction or dissatisfaction. An obvious bias in most studies is suggested by their focus on assembly-line workers—a vital part of the auto work force, but actually less than 20 percent of the total blue-collar force. Even in assembly plants (which are a minority of the factories in the auto industry) about one-third of the employees (material handlers, maintenance, skilled trades) do not work on the line. Widick's breakdown of General Motors employment and job classification figures illuminates this point. Consequently, the generally accepted stereotype of the auto industry worker, Charlie Chaplin's man on the assembly line, which is still accepted, is misleading, for it distorts as well as fails to portray the problems of most auto workers.

On the concept of "alienation" the participants agreed with Robert Reiff that "the general claims of alienation and dehumanization are exaggerated and misleading" (see first paragraphs of his article). He questions the usage of the term "alienation," which varies depending on the observer's background and discipline and traces back to Marx's theories on the conflict between capital and workers.

The concepts of "job satisfaction" or of "alienation" do not offer a satisfactory explanation for the degree of conflict, change, or challenge found in the workplace environment. Studies based on those concepts do not explain the existence of the auto union, its impact, and its struggles, or the problems growing out of the heterogeneous and changing composition of the work force, or the effect of social, economic, and political events on the work force.

As Henry Ford II remarked in 1972, "Much of the auto industry work is boring, but that is also true of factory jobs in many industries." Yet some researchers have found that workers on boring jobs are satisfied with them. One reason for this is that when workers consider being unemployed as a very real alternative brought home to them by the current recession, the job they are holding appears much less unsatisfactory. Compared to less desirable jobs (coal mining is an example), even the toughest auto assembly-line jobs are considered preferable. Daniel Bell stressed the question of comparison when he wrote, "Unless sociologists give the worker an alternative job to compare his present job with, the questions about job satisfaction represent neither 'meaningful' nor 'real choices.'"

These general considerations prompted the participants to take the approach that looking at visible and identifiable sources of discontent in concrete circumstances offered the best explanations of work and its discontents in the auto industry, rather than becoming mired in metaphysical concepts of "satisfaction" or "alienation."

Speedup, of course, remains a chronic and frequently an acute problem, as the participants reaffirmed. Currently it has been superseded by job insecurity, which has always been a persistent source of anxiety and tension in auto plants. Between layoffs in the six postwar recessions, including the devastations produced by the 1974-75 cutbacks, plant closings, production and shift changes, and fear of job loss due to automation, auto workers seldom have a sense of stability on the job.

Also ignored or underestimated in most studies is the whole issue of working conditions as sources of conflict and discontent, discussed by Widick in Chapter 1. Problems of health, safety, and unpleasant conditions such as noise, heat, and fumes have always been the major reasons for grievances and wildcat strikes. But until the entire environment became a subject of national debate in the 1970's, the working environment in the auto and other industrial plants was largely ignored in the surveys and books about the quality of work in this industry. (See Al Nash's comments in his literature on the quality of work in the auto industry.)

In talking about "dissatisfaction" too much attention has been paid to the statistical artifact, "the average worker." A great deviation from the norm is to be found among auto workers in their level of dissatisfaction. Some find work satisfactory. Others are as turned off as young counterculturists. We have focused on the most important variables: age obviously is significant, and young workers are more dissatisfied; race is highly significant.

The tensions between blacks and whites in auto plants is at a high peak due to the social polarization occurring in American society over questions like busing or job rights in a period of recession. Sex is also significant, but probably less than other variables. Women are more dissatisfied than men, but do not reach the intensity of anger felt by the blacks.

Because a large part of the total work force is required to work second shift, a normal family life or living condition is excluded. Currently in the auto industry these aggravations are intensified by the fears among many workers over the use of drugs by workers, a situation both the UAW and the auto industry deny is serious, contrary to all the reports and interviews Widick received as late as April 1975.

Until the 1974-75 recession, the issue of compulsory overtime had assumed significant proportions, reflected in the debate over the question in national bargaining. The lack of any individual choice for the worker has been demeaning.

The never-ending resistance to accepting management rules or the conditions of work testify to the fact that auto workers have not been turned into robots or been dehumanized. Quite the contrary, workers often exert their own form of control and independence through doubling up, banking work, developing shortcuts, regulating output—to mention a few activities. They often violate the collective bargaining agreement through wildcat strikes, pressure on the union, changing stewards and committeemen in the plant, quitting, staying home, slowing down, griping, and grieving.

Not all of these forms of human assertion are necessarily formal grievances unless so labeled by the collective bargaining agreement. Consequently, formal grievances are only partial reflections of the sense of injustice workers frequently feel on the job. Earning ''good'' money still remains the major reason why people work in auto plants and put up with the difficulties. Unquestionably, as a Ford management report indicated in 1969 and as the Lordstown strike emphasized in 1973, young workers remain the most discontented group among auto workers. This is reflected in their critical attitude toward the union, quits, discharges, "illegitimate" actions on the job, and job discipline.

Most studies have ignored the impact of the union on the life of auto workers and at the workplace: (1) As a bargaining agent the union has been successful in obtaining a variety of benefits unparalleled in the private sector. The individual worker does not have to bargain with a giant corporation by himself. He has an organized expression of his views. (2) The creation of a permanent structure for grievance handling, with whatever deficiencies it may have, has resulted in giving a degree of redress not available to most blue-collar workers in America. For example, as indicated earlier, in General Motors alone, the union processes an average of two hundred fifty thousand grievances annually. (3) The success of the union is input due to the introduction of the "just cause" concept at the union's insistence in dealing with discharges and discipline, which is a far superior form of human relations than the "straw boss" picture of the foreman in the preunion days. (4) The collective bargaining agreement regulates or moderates conflict, but does not eliminate it. The right to engage in conflict, which is legitimated and protected by the collective bargaining agreement and the presence of the union, permits the workers to exercise some degree of control over their quality of working life and, consequently, to mitigate the severity of the line, the harshness of working conditions, and the authoritarian rule of the management.

Man-made decisions rather than the machine (technology) are the source of problems and disputes in the auto industry. Prerogatives of management that allow it to compel compulsory overtime, control transfers, close plants, set the speed of the line, and determine working conditions (including safety and health) are major determinants in creating dissatisfaction and unrest among workers and in maintaining the authority and power of management.

The function of the union (UAW) essentially has been to modify this unilateral control and power through the collective bargaining process, which ends in the signing of a contract on wages, hours, and working conditions. The union functions as an alleviative force. Its plant bargaining is within the constraints of the contracts and defined in the grievance procedure. Unquestionably, this is far superior to the domination of the work force in unorganized plants by management, bound from being unlimited only by national law and union competition. More specifically, as Sexton has noted in a private letter:

> The quality of interaction in many work situations is something special in the working world—often warm, intense, outspoken. While the jobs themselves might tend to call on the robot-like, automated responses of workers, the interrelationships in the plant have a dramatically opposite effect. These interactions have a profoundly humanizing effect on many workers.
>
> Indeed, it sometimes seems to me that the most important contribution the union makes in the shop is in its impact on these interactions. The union increases them, intensifies them, makes them more meaningful, gives them purpose. It gives people something important to "share in common." It gives them something to talk about. It helps them to think together about their own condition. It gives them direction, incentive, experience in working together toward solution of common problems.
>
> The union's impact on people has been far more significant than its impact on the company or on the democratization of industry generally.
>
> While the UAW has had dramatic successes in collective bargaining, and while these successes have greatly diminished the individual worker's sense of helplessness and "alienation," what becomes increasingly obvious is not how far this most progressive union has come, but how far it has to go. The grievance machinery in particular, which is at the heart of the bargaining contract, is clearly in need of massive overhaul. So ineffective and lethargic is the process in most places that workers are increasingly turning to the courts—which are themselves notoriously slow—to win legal and contractual rights.
>
> The union needs to do more "master planning." It needs more creative thinking, especially in relationship to issues of (1) control of industrial decision-making and ownership and (2) work satisfaction. It needs to move into issues beyond pay, conditions, fringe benefits, as vital as these issues have been.

In our combined experience, the participants concluded that the union plays a significant role in transforming industrial autocracy into a more modern and reasonable set of rules governing relations between blue-collar workers and the company, but much remains to be done, as our summary of the discontents in this paper suggests.

Finally, in our experience and study we found no evidence that the auto workers are either robots or dehumanized, nor are they a combination of satisfied robots and ignorant Archie Bunkers. Their prejudices and general outlook reflect those of other segments of American society.

They do have a grievance against society, with its middle-class values, and that is the general contempt in which factory workers, in particular assembly-line workers, are held, making it doubly difficult for blue-collar workers to maintain a sense of personal pride and dignity. Even skilled workers in auto plants often feel superior to the assembly-line or unskilled worker. And those who see workers as robots or Archie Bunkers also contribute to the antagonisms, irritations, and frustrations of the people who work for a living in the auto factories.

Professor B. J. Widick
Columbia University

Professor Al Nash
Cornell University

Professor Robert Reiff
Albert Einstein School
    of Medicine

Professor Patricia Cayo Sexton
New York University

Bill Goode
Associate Dean
Empire State Labor College

Epilogue:
Working Conditions and Managements' Interests

by Ivar Berg

Debate over the nature and implications of "work in America" has been marked by inconclusiveness. One may go back to Thorstein Veblen's chapter "On the Nature and Uses of Sabotage" in *The Engineer and the Price System*, first published in 1921, to Stanley Mathewson's *Restriction of Output Among Unorganized Workers*, published in 1931, to the 1929 Hawthorne Experiments by Harvard Business School professors, or to studies under the aegis of the National Commission on Productivity in the 1970's and find some of the same ambiguities discussed by Widick and his colleagues in the pages of this volume.

The data on the subject simply do not enable us to reach "clean" and definitive conclusions about work and workers' reactions. This fact emerges very clearly from the recollections and assessments in the present volume, as do a number of the reasons for the difficulties in interpreting available data. Thus, differences in methods and in the assumptions of investigators are prominent among the obstacles to unambiguous interpretations, differences that are explored by the former auto workers with sensitivity, feeling, and some considerable social science savvy.

It may be useful as an epilogue, however, to consider the deficiencies in the data on the *consequences* of work experiences in the United States, as well as those in the *adaptations* and *attitudes* of workers described in earlier chapters. The former data are highly deficient. Discovering the reasons may help us to understand why remediable problems in the workplace are the subject of such essentially trivial efforts, either public or private, to correct the abuses, the discomforts, and the difficulties itemized by the authors of the present volume.

To the extent that data on the consequences and correlates of work methods *are* available—on labor force participation rates, work attendance, quit rates, productivity, alcohol and drug use, industrial conflict (contrast rejections, strikes, grievance and arbitration cases), and on intraunion matters (changes in union leadership, decertification elections)—they show little evidence of increasing worker discontent.[1] The "behavioral" data, like much if not most of the other ore mined by investigators in this area, as Nash suggests, assays very poorly; in common with our debased dollar, our intellectual currency here proves to be of very problematical value.[2]

The *deficiencies* in each of the time series dealing with workers' behavior, I submit, are far better indicators of the remarkably low degree of *managers'* concerns with the problems of workers, described so feelingly in the papers by Widick and his colleagues in this volume, than are the data themselves in identifying areas requiring intervention!

Consider that the rational manager contemplated in textbooks would be hard put to make reasonable and economically fruitful decisions in any of the areas of work experience to which "behavioral" data refer. Indeed, the pitiful condition of social-economic data on workers—most of whom are not even covered in data that describe only manufacturing workers—calls to mind the enduringly marginal, if not downright pathetic role of personnel administrators in most employment settings in this country. No competent observer of the scene in Western Europe, meantime, could fail to note the assiduousness with which such statistics are pursued where full employment, earlier experiences with inflation (in short, the marketplace), and a disciplined communist movement have forced more realistic assessments of manpower experiences.[3] Ironically, and in line with Sexton's discussion, it is the government, in our system, and not the marketplace, that will facilitate *some* improvement in manpower data, for firms will be obliged, in response to affirmative action requirements, to attend to the quality of data that must inform *all* aspects of manpower utilization in the enterprise.

The last observation is relevant in any effort to answer the question of *why* the statistics we refer to are so deficient. The partial insulation of firms from the chill winds of the marketplace by such "shelters" as tax credits, rapid depreciation write-offs, and unemployment, clearly is *a* factor. But there are others.

One possibility, of course, is that such data are embarrassing to managers. Few knowledgeable observers will deny, for example, that grievance and strike data—especially data on "wildcats"—are understated by the principals involved. No industrial relations vice president enjoys acknowledging whatever failures might have fed "quickie strikes"; ditto shop stewards, "reps," and local union presidents. Drug and alcohol studies are, of course, resisted by all, raising as they do sensitive questions of employees' privacy no less than of employers' insurance rates. These and similar reasons for faulty social statistics in the work arena are as valid as they are understandable, at least from one point of view. From another perspective, they literally invite the explanation that the work experiences to which such data point are simply *not important enough* to require careful human and manpower accounting.

That the economic wastes, even ignoring the individual discomforts and human losses, of badly managed work are of a lower order of concern than well-intentioned social scientists, among others, might wish, is the most logical inference to be drawn from a discussion by Richard Walton, director of research at the Harvard Business School. Presented at an American Assembly on The Changing World of Work, his discussion can be instructively juxtaposed with the one to which the authors of the present volume contributed. His task was to consider the condition of eleven of the best-known efforts to improve the lot of workers through work redesign and work enlargement experiments of the types to which Nash has made references.

Three of these, Walton reports, "have returned to conventional patterns. . . . Many others have regressed somewhat after a few years. . . . Several other innovative plants . . . are still successful and evolving in the direction that they were launched." [4]

Among the plants in the third group he includes the General Foods pet food (Gainesburger) plant in Topeka, Kansas, the validity of claims about which Walton can assure us because he was "closely involved as a consultant." The reader may gauge, for him or herself the degree to which an enthusiastic proponent of work restructuring, one who makes some of his annual income in direct connection with such ventures, will likely be an objective commentator on the reasons for successes, failures, or "regressions."

The only internal evidence of a lack of scientific detachment, apart from a failure to mention that the Topeka operation replaced a unionized plant in Kankakee, Illinois (!), stems from Walton's curiously uncritical reactions to the reasons for failure and backsliding that he has, himself, pinpointed and reported with great if somewhat unwitting candor. Such an uncritical reaction could as well be evidence of ingenuousness as of "involvement" or other blocks to objectivity.

Thus, he does not see, in the aggregate, a *contradiction* between the presumably desirable and humane objectives of work redesigners and those of career managers who fail, according to Walton, to gain support from top executives. He reports on the oversights of managers who failed to follow through on efforts that had raised the expectations of employees participating in experiments; who were unwilling to reduce supervision "and materially increase workers' influence in critical decisions," despite the experimentally reduced *needs* for traditional controls; who failed to reduce turnover to a threshold level (10 percent) beyond which a requisite "bank of necessary skills" is too depleted for the redesigned and "enlarged" work to be effectively executed;[5] who accepted new appointments and thereby drained the pool of qualified, trained, and committed successors; who lost their consultants to other clients; who could not *"contend"* with the expansion of work to be performed by the relevant work unit, or by the larger plant; who could not maintain a "steady state" in the experimental operation when

99

"pressures developed" for greater "predictability . . . and certainty" and for "less movement of personnel, more specialization among workers, and closer supervision."[6]

Already we note, in this partial enumeration of Walton's "subversive" factors, that these innovative "restructurings" of work may well be ground up in the dialectics of the enterprise. They are dependent upon many of the very conditions they are, themselves, designed to produce! But the author refers vaguely to the issue listed last in the previous paragraph, for example, as attributable to "technical problems" which, according to his informant, "induced a certain amount of unexpected stress in the social system." One is left with the very strong impression that a revolution in managerial thinking and behavior—*all* of its thinking—is the most important condition for long-term successes in the redesign of work, a revolution that would have implications even for the way markets operate.

This impression is significantly reinforced when Walton alludes to other aspects of the functions of the executive. Keeping in mind the discussion in the present volume, consider the following revealing statement:

> Two of these companies came under new, severe, and long-term competitive pressures that resulted in new initiatives and influence patterns emanating from the top. Higher management began emphasizing cost reduction and near-term results, insisting upon discipline and compliance with their programs, and in general providing an inhospitable environment for the innovative work system.
>
> Authoritarian decisions and "do it" commands tended to erase the premise that a subordinate could freely challenge superiors in unguarded dialogue. Politically-based influence techniques undermined the premise that a person's influence would be a function of his expertise and information. And, as cliques formed to exercise influence, interpersonal relationships were corrupted, trust was eroded, and the sense of "community" began to deteriorate.[7]

Little in the foregoing catalogue of what was once called "bureaupathologies" is strange to most students of administration and management, be they in firms, sociology departments, or consultants' offices.

Nor is it new that favorable local agreements between workers and managers in an experimental setting will, as Walton complains, form part of more general contract negotiations in the company's and union's other locations in which productivity gains have, for whatever reasons, been slower and in which the parties have different problems in confronting the production process.

We have already seen in Walton's evidence that managers are not a homogeneous group of what would ultimately look very much like an aggregation of old-fashioned syndicalists. Even if they each approximated the "types" implied by Walton's assessment to be required in innovative firms, it will surprise many readers less than it did Walton that higher-paid workers in an experimental setting will reduce their psychological investments in work redesign when their peers, in other company settings, gradually receive the benefits previously accorded only to those who have "allowed (management) the freedom necessary to conduct the experiment."[8]

"Consider," writes Walton solemnly, "the implications of the last statement . . . . It suggests that the equity concept is so strong that even though employees may be intrinsically rewarded by taking on high responsibility and making high contributions, their extrinsic reward must also be in line with their relatively high work inputs. If this is not the case, their sense of injustice will cause them to scale down their level of involvement."[9]

The difficulties in all this are almost insurmountable, judging from Walton's list of the additional conditions "favorable to pilot project implementation" revealed by his study. These are outlined on page 161:

(1) Small towns. "They provide a community context and a work force that is more amenable to the innovation."

(2) Small work forces.

(3) New plants. "It is easier to change employees' deeply ingrained expectations about work and management in a new plant culture."

(4) Geographic separation of the experimental unit from other parts of the firm's facilities.

(5) "The use of outside consultants as change agents provides objectivity and know-how."

(6) A significant factor in several cases: long lead teams, implicit in start-ups, allow large blocks of time for the "training and acculturation" of participants.

(7) No unions, or where union-management relations are "positive."

These conditions are not easily met, as may be plainly seen, and some of them may, like reduced turnover, be as much a desired *result* of a successful effort as a condition for its success. Thus, the former chairman of the National Commission on Productivity, Ted Mills, addressing the last of Walton's seven conditions, reported to participants in an earlier conference on The Changing Work Ethic, from a private corporation survey, that 80 percent of 150 work experiments meeting minimum criteria for inclusion in the study were undertaken specifically to *avoid* unions.

That managers as employers of "human capital" may consider this resource either not worth husbanding or too difficult to husband, meantime, reasonably may be inferred from two companion studies funded by the Department of Labor. The results are critical to an understanding of managers' willingness to be passive or negative toward the problem of work in America, basic employer reactions Walton simply gainsays in his discussion of the depressing failures, the slippages, "the politics," and all the rest of the realities he describes so articulately.

In the first of these studies, Daniel Diamond and Brach Bedrosian investigated the role of hiring standards among employers in the development of "labor market imbalances." To this end, they examined ten major entry and "near-entry" jobs in each of five white-collar and four blue-collar occupations, together with one service occupation, in the New York and St. Louis Standard Metropolitan Statistical Areas. These data represented fourteen industry groups and included twenty samples of establishments—one for each of the ten occupations surveyed in each of these SMSAs. They reported that though hiring requirements were quite specific, they were unrelated to job performance across cities, industries, or companies. In seventeen of the twenty categories there was little or no difference in job performance attributable to differences in workers' educational achievements. Material differences between hiring standards and real job requirements were, however, associated with and "appeared to be an important cause of costly turnover in a major segment" of the firms "in virtually all of the twenty groups." [10]

In the second study, by H. G. Heneman, Jr., and George Seltzer, the focus was on the approaches to manpower planning and forecasting of sixty-nine Minnesota firms employing more than five hundred workers and on the techniques they employed to those ends. [11]

Half of the firms did no forecasting of their manpower requirements, and only a third forecast manpower available! Nearly 20 percent of the firms had begun forecasting activities only one year before. Of the firms that did *some* forecasting in this costly area, "sales" were the only determining factor considered by over one-half; about 90 percent used forecasts for recruiting, but only one-third related manpower forecasts to budget plans, training, or transfer and promotion programs; only one-tenth used the forecasts in plans for production, space, and facilities; and their use in plans for acquisition and expansion or in product pricing was reported even *less* frequently. "In brief," report the investigators, "manpower seemed to be almost completely isolated from other types of planning." Twenty percent of the manufacturing firms in this sample had no occupational breakdown on employment, 30 percent had none on separations and hires, and 60 percent had none on age. [12]

In a feasibility study involving five hundred manufacturing firms by the Bureau of Labor Statistics, designed to determine whether deficiencies in national "absenteeism" data could be remedied through the use of employer data on absenteeism, it was found that "fewer than two-fifths of all workers worked in firms keeping records on absences." [13] That study reports that only 40 percent of the firms, many quite independent of their experiences about absenteeism, considered unscheduled absence among production workers a "very serious" or "moderate'' problem; less than one-seventh of these five hundred employers applied such descriptions to unscheduled absences among their white-collar employees.

These investigations are relevant to conclusions about work in America because they help to inform us about the perspectives within which manpower management problems are viewed by *employers*. They suggest, very strongly, that manpower problems do not stand in a prominent place on the agendas of those who should, by all logic, be most concerned about them. The fact helps considerably, furthermore, in explaining the dreary if familiar processes Walton describes as subversive of innovative experiments in the workplace. I will not review the reasons why manpower concerns are not principal ones among managers, a topic well attended by the competent ''managerialists'' and ''behaviorists'' who sought in the 1940's and early 1950's to recast the model of the firm handed down by microeconomists. It is sufficient to say that the ''recasters'' focused, quite realistically, on the potent roles of unemployment and of market imperfections in their studies of the forces that contributed to what might be called management irrationality. [14]

We need not argue that all managers are simply cynical, as the foregoing discussion hints. Like union leaders who are skeptical of ''quick solutions,'' there are many managers who recognize complexity for what it is. As the authors of the present volume sensibly insist, auto workers, like other workers, are a heterogeneous lot with a complicated mosaic of interests, circumstances that *compel* inconclusive, and ambiguous assessments.

The fact is that work reforms with putatively humanitarian consequences are likely to unsettle the status quo in production and related organizations. Observers do not often see the status quo—let's call it the social contract—for what it is, a *system* of arrangements, procedures, methods, and work rules that has been hammered out over time and involves long lists of bargains, adjustments, accommodations, and agreements. These lead to job classifications and other elements of social and organizational predictability in which *both* workers and managers have considerable investments, including ones that are vaguely and intractably psychological as well as more fundamentally and concretely "economic." They may not be written off by well-intentioned third parties as simply "politics" or the result of "Luddite" attitudes.[15] Efficiency and productivity gains are *among* the ends of managers; they are not the only ends. Stability, predictability, and collaboration also rank high among organizational "consummations devoutly to be wished."

No competent student of industrial relations, experienced in the field, would fail to note that work has often been "enlarged," "enriched," and otherwise "restructured" *by workers and their immediate supervisors*, as some of Widick's colleagues, especially Bill Goode, imply in the pages of this book. The "work rules" that result from these negotiations are often criticized as protecting "featherbedding," however, when they have not been introduced by consultants from the "behavioral sciences" who collect substantial fees for helping to "humanize work."

The inclination to compare contemporary Western European developments toward the "humanization" of work invidiously with those in the United States, meantime, ought to be resisted. There are gross differences in positions and prospects regarding employee well-being between the American and non-American cases stemming from the many differences in the political, social, and economic histories of the United States and the Western European nations.

These differences, too numerous to recapitulate in this context, point to the gross differences in the respective roles of unions, in the rights of managers, and in the more profound philosophical premises that inform "industrial democracy" as a working concept in the "old" and "new" worlds. The strategic political significance of trade unions in England, Germany, Norway, Sweden, and, in large measure, France has (1) led to extraordinary elaborations on Bismarckian reforms; (2) "nationalized" many issues still bargained over in the United States by separate unions and companies; (3) made faulty manpower decisions very costly to West European employers who pay high severance costs and who must "bank" parts of retained earnings in state depositories. Unions have considerable influence over the conditions under which the funds, in the last of these items, are to be spent.

In passing, one may note that almost all of Western Europe's economies, conceived as advanced industrial apparatuses, have not even reached their twenty-fifth birthdays. In a sense we are prisoners, in the United States, of an industrial relations system, of a system of employee-employer relations, and of a slower evolutionary process that has not forced and crystallized questions to which the work innovations in Western Europe's "social democracies" have been responsive. In all this, many Western European nations have been aided (or harmed, depending upon one's viewpoints of management's rights and of the reasons for inflation) by exceedingly high levels of employment, which in several nations in Europe, until most recently, facilitated (yes, even necessitated) reforms of all types in the workplace.

We may state, by way of conclusions, that workers will indeed vary in the degree of their outrage and irritation with the quality of working life in their employment settings, as the former auto workers insist and demonstrate in their several contributions. Their experiences and the data on attitudes they review confirm the heterogeneous responses to jobs that tend, in general, as they point out, to be unappealing.

We can add that workers will strive to cope with their circumstances, as the authors emphasize with some pride, by the applications of what Veblen called, collectively, "strategies of independence." Their heterogeneous interests (and mixed fears) assure that these "strategies" will no more be of one piece than will be their grievances, large and small.

Just as clear, however, is the conclusion of this epilogue that employers are not much disturbed by the cost—organizational or human—that accompanies working conditions in America. This lack of concern is demonstrated, on one side, by the deficiencies in relevant data and, on the other, by the temporal, even ephemeral quality of management's interests in potentially cost-reducing efforts to reform the conditions that evoke Veblen's "strategies of independence." Workers, no less than managers, meantime, are mindful of the extraordinarily important role of business cycles and their effects on labor markets in shaping worker demands and employer responses.

Notes

1. Similar conclusions regarding worker attitudes are reported in a review of surveys in Robert Quinn et al., *Job Satisfaction: Is There a Trend?*, Manpower Research Monograph No. 30, U.S. Department of Labor, Manpower Administration (Washington, D.C.: U.S. Government Printing Office, 1974).

2. For a detailed discussion, see Peter Henle, "Economic Effects," in Jerome M. Rosow, ed., *The Worker and the Job: Coping with Change* (Englewood Cliffs, N.J.: Prentice-Hall, 1974), pp. 119–44.

3. For a fine discussion, see James W. Kuhn, *Bargaining in the Grievance Process* (New York: Columbia University Press, 1961). It should be noted that most of Widick's data on grievances and the rest, presented in this volume, had to be gathered "privately."

4. Richard E. Walton, "Innovative Restructuring of Work," in Rosow, ed., *Worker and the Job*, pp. 145–76.

5. Walton reports that, in one experiment, turnover exceeded 10 percent because, according to an informant, "of the existence of unusual opportunities for overseas assignments." It is interesting to note that such experiments are in part undertaken to *reduce* turnover, a fact that raises questions about the degree to which working conditions must be viewed in the context of competent labor market analysis. Work reforms that take no account of the firm's *own* internal labor market's functioning are simply naive. Just as naive are reforms introduced at one point in a firm's competitive history that take no account of the firm's changing experiences in product markets.

6. Walton, "Innovative Restructuring," p. 167.

7. Ibid., p. 168. For a concrete illustration the reader may refer to the Lordstown case, discussed earlier in the present volume.

8. Ibid., p. 169. Compare Walton's apparent surprise with the discussions, in this volume, of the extraordinary diversity of worker motives and the intramural conflicts among workers' interests.

9. Ibid., p. 169.

10. Daniel E. Diamond and Brach Bedrosian, *Hiring Standards and Job Performance*, Manpower Research Monograph No. 18, U.S. Department of Labor (Washington, D.C.: U.S. Government Printing Office, 1970). These estimates are entirely in line with those by the author. See Ivar Berg, *Education and Jobs: The Great Training Robbery* (New York: Praeger, 1970).

11. H. G. Heneman, Jr., and George Seltzer, *Employer Manpower Planning and Forecasting*, Manpower Research Monograph No. 19, U.S. Department of Labor (Washington, D.C.: U.S. Government Printing Office, 1970).

12. By 1974 all but small firms must "track" such data for purposes of compliance with equal opportunity requirements.

13. J. H. Hedges, "Absences from Work," *Monthly Labor Review*, 96 (1973): 24–25.

14. For a helpful summary of the issues that divided what he regarded as the warring factions in 1948, see Fritz Machlup's 1966 Presidential Address to the American Economics Association, "Theories of the Firm: Marginalist, Behavioral, Managerial," *American Economic Review*, 57 (March 1967): 1–33.

15. "Luddites" were *not* resisting technical change. These English workers broke "frames" in the period 1814–20 because their employers reduced workers' wages to pay rents on the mules, frames, and jennies to those who "put out" raw materials and whose markets for cotton textiles were sealed off by Napoleon's "Continental System." Rent increases replaced the market gains of "putters out" and came from workers' pockets.

Biographical Notes

B. J. Widick, M.A., is professor of industrial relations, Graduate School of Business, Columbia University. He was employed in an auto plant for fifteen years, during which he was elected chief steward and committeeman for ten years. His books include: *The UAW and Walter Reuther* (Random House) with Irving Howe, *Labor Today, the Triumphs and Failures of Unionism in the U.S.A.* (Houghton-Mifflin), and *Detroit: City of Race and Class Violence* (Quadrangle Books). Since 1958 he has been labor correspondent of *The Nation* magazine.

Bill Goode, M.A., associate dean of Empire State Labor College, State University of New York, worked for ten years in auto plants, going through the skilled trades apprentice program, being a journeyman pipefitter, a shop committeeman, and an education director of the United Auto Workers.

Al Nash, Ph.D., associate professor of sociology New York State School of Industrial and Labor Relations, Cornell University, worked four years in an aircraft plant, then six years in two auto plants. He was a chief steward, a local union president, and a staff representative.

Robert Reiff, Ph.D., is professor and director of the Center for the Study of Social Intervention of the Albert Einstein College of Medicine. He worked for three years as a welder on the metal shop assembly line and was an elected chief steward.

Patricia Cayo Sexton, Ph.D., a professor of sociology at New York University, spent four years as an assembly-line worker and was an elected full-time chief steward at the Dodge Main plant.

Bibliography

by Al Nash

Aronowitz, Stanley. *False Promises: The Shaping of the American Working Class.* New York: McGraw-Hill, 1974.

Bell, Daniel. "Work, Alienation, and Social Control," *Dissent,* 21 (Spring 1974): 207-12.

———. *Work and Its Discontents.* Boston: Beacon Press, 1956.

Berger, Bennett. *Working-Class Suburb.* Berkeley: University of California Press, 1960.

Blauner, Robert. *Alienation and Freedom: The Factory Worker and His Industry.* Chicago: University of Chicago Press, 1964.

———. "Work Satisfaction and Industrial Trends in Modern Society," pp. 339-60 in W. Galenson and S. M. Lipset, eds., *Labor and Trade Unionism.* New York: John Wiley and Sons, 1960.

Bluestone, Irving. "Worker Participation in Decision-Making," pp. 49-61 in Roy F. Fairfield, ed., *Humanizing the Workplace.* Buffalo: Prometheus Books, 1974.

Braverman, Harry. *Labor and Monopoly Capital: The Degradation of Work in the Twentieth Century.* New York: Monthly Review Press, 1974.

Chinoy, Eli. *Automobile Workers and the American Dream.* Boston: Beacon Press, 1955.

———. "Manning the Machines—The Assembly Line Worker," pp. 51-81 in Peter L. Berger, ed., *The Human Shape of Work.* New York: Macmillan Co., 1964.

Coser, Lewis A. *The Functions of Social Conflict.* Glencoe, Ill.: Free Press, 1956.

Dunn, Robert W. *Labor and Automobiles.* New York: International Publishers, 1929.

109

Faunce, William A. "Automation in the Automobile Industry: Some Consequences for the Plant Social Structure," *American Sociological Review*, 23 (August 1958): 401-2.

———. "The Automobile Industry: A Case Study in Automation," pp. 44-53 in H. B. Jacobson and J. S. Roucek, eds., *Automation and Society*. New York: Philosophical Library, 1959.

———. *Problems of Industrial Society*. New York: McGraw-Hill, 1969.

Form, William H. "Auto Workers and Their Machines: A Study of Work, Factory, and Job Satisfaction in Four Countries," *Social Forces*, 52 (September 1973): 1-15.

———. "The Internal Stratification of the Working Class: Involvements of Auto Workers in Four Countries," *American Sociological Review*, 38 (December 1973): 696-711.

———. "Technology and Social Behavior in Four Countries: A Sociotechnical Perspective," *American Sociological Review*, 37 (December 1972): 727-38.

Fountain, Clayton W. *Union Guy*. New York: Harcourt and Brace, 1949.

Fullan, Michael. "Industrial Technology and Worker Integration in the Organization," *American Sociological Review*, 35 (December 1970): 1028-39.

Goldthorpe, John. "Attitudes and Behavior of Car Assembly Workers: A Deviant Case and a Theoretical Critique," *British Journal of Sociology*, 17 (September 1966): 227-44.

Gooding, Judson. "Blue-Collar Blues on the Assembly Line," *Fortune*, July 1970.

Guest, Robert H. "The Man on the Assembly Line: A Generation Later," *Tuck Today* (May 1973), 1-8.

———. "Men and Machines," Reprint from *Personnel* (May 1955), 1-8.

———. "Work Careers and Aspirations of Automobile Workers," pp. 319-28 in W. Galenson and S. M. Lipset, eds., *Labor and Trade Unionism*. New York: John Wiley and Sons, 1960.

Harris, Herbert. *American Labor*. New Haven: Yale University Press, 1938.

Herzberg, Frederick, Bernard Mausner, and Barbara Bloch Synderman. *The Motivation to Work*. New York: John Wiley and Sons, 1959.

Howe, Irving, and B. J. Widick. *The UAW and Walter Reuther*. New York: Random House, 1949.

Katzell, Raymond, et al. "Work, Productivity, and Job Satisfaction: An Evaluation of Policy-Related Research, Part 1 and Part 2." New York: New York University, unpublished.

Kornhauser, Arthur. *Mental Health of the Industrial Worker*. New York: John Wiley and Sons, 1965.

Kraus, Henry. *The Many and the Few.* Los Angeles: Plantin Press, 1946.

Kreman, Bennett. "Search for a Better Way of Work: Lordstown, Ohio," in Roy P. Fairfield, ed., *Humanizing the Workplace.* Buffalo: Prometheus Books, 1974.

Kruchko, John G. *The Birth of a Local Union: The History of UAW Local 674, Norwood, Ohio, 1933-1940.* Ithaca: New York State School of Industrial and Labor Relations, Cornell University, 1962.

Levison, Andrew. *The Working Class Majority.* New York: Coward, McCann, and Geoghegan, 1974.

Marquart, Frank. "The Auto Worker," pp. 143-57 in *Voices of Dissent.* New York: Grove Press, 1958.

———."New Problems for the Unions," *Dissent,* 6 (Autumn 1959): 375-88.

———."Trouble in Auto," *Dissent,* 8 (Spring 1961): 112-15.

Mott, Paul E., et al. *Shift Work: The Social, Psychological and Physical Consequences.* Ann Arbor: University of Michigan Press, 1965.

Nash, Al. "Attitudes of Unions toward Work and Leisure." Typescript, 1969.

Rosenberg, Bernard. "Torn Apart and Driven Together: Portrait of a UAW Local in Chicago," *Dissent,* 19 (Winter 1972): 61-69.

———."The UAW: An Aura of Hope," *Dissent,* 14 (July-August 1967): 390-97.

Rothschild, Emma. *Paradise Lost: The Decline of the Auto-Industrial Age.* New York: Vintage Books, 1974.

Salpukas, Andrew. "Unions: A New Role?" pp. 99-118 in Jerome M. Rosow, ed., *The Worker and the Job: Coping with Change.* Englewood Cliffs, N.J.: Prentice Hall, 1974.

Serrin, William. *The Company and the Union.* New York: Alfred A. Knopf, 1973.

Sexton, Patricia Cayo, and Brendon Sexton. *Blue Collar and Hard Hats.* New York: Random House, 1971.

Shelley, E. F., and Co. *Climbing the Job Ladder.* New York: E. F. Shelley and Co., 1970.

Shepard, Jon. "Functional Specialization and Work Attitudes," *Industrial Relations,* 8 (February 1969): 185-94.

Siassi, Iradj, Guido Crocetti, and Herzl R. Spiro. "Loneliness and Dissatisfaction in a Blue Collar Population," *Archives of General Psychiatry,* 30 (February 1974): 261-65.

Strauss, George. "Workers: Attitudes and Adjustments," in Jerome M. Rosow, ed., *The Worker and the Job: Coping with Change.* Englewood Cliffs, N.J.: Prentice Hall, 1974.

Swados, Harvey. "The Myth of the Happy Worker," pp. 106-13 in E. and M. Josephson, eds., *Man Alone.* New York: Dell, 1962.
———."The UAW—Over the Top or Over the Hill," *Dissent,* 10 (Autumn 1963): 321-43.
U.S. Department of Health, Education, and Welfare. *Work in America: Report of a Special Task Force to the Secretary of Health, Education, and Welfare.* Cambridge, Mass.: MIT Press, 1973.
Vorse, Mary H. *Labor's New Millions.* New York: Modern Age Books, 1938.
Walker, Charles, and Robert Guest. *The Man on the Assembly Line.* Cambridge, Mass.: Harvard University Press, 1952.
Wallick, Frank. *The American Worker: An Endangered Species.* New York: Ballantine Books, 1972.
Widick, B. J. *Labor Today.* Cambridge, Mass.: Houghton Mifflin Co., 1964.
———."The UAW: Limitations of Unionism," *Dissent,* 6 (Autumn 1959): 446-53.

Library of Congress Cataloging in Publication Data

Main entry under title:

Auto work and its discontents.

    (Policy studies in employment and welfare ; no. 25)
    Bibliography: p. 109.
      1. Automobile industry workers—United States—
Addresses, essays, lectures. 2. Job satisfaction—
United States—Addresses, essays, lectures. 3. Assembly-
line methods—Addresses, essays, lectures. I. Widick,
B. J.
HD8039.A82U624   331.7'62'92220973   76-16095
ISBN 0-8018-1856-7
ISBN 0-8018-1857-5 pbk.